INSTRUCTOR'S RESOURCE MANUAL WITH VIDEO GUIDE

Tara Radin
University of Virginia

FUNDAMENTALS OF MANAGEMENT

Stephen P. Robbins
San Diego State University

David A. De Cenzo
Towson State University

PRENTICE HALL
Englewood Cliffs, New Jersey 07632

Project manager: Nancy Proyect
Acquisitions editor: Natalie Anderson
Associate editor: Lisamarie Brassini
Manufacturing buyer: Ken Clinton

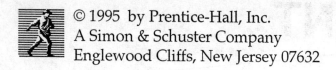

Printed in the United States of America

10 9 8 7 6 5 4 3 2 1

ISBN 0-13-307273-8

Prentice-Hall International (UK) Limited, *London*
Prentice-Hall of Australia Pty. Limited, *Sydney*
Prentice-Hall Canada Inc., *Toronto*
Prentice-Hall Hispanoamericana, S.A., *Mexico*
Prentice-Hall of India Private Limited, *New Delhi*
Prentice-Hall of Japan, Inc., *Tokyo*
Simon & Schuster Asia Pte. Ltd., *Singapore*
Editora Prentice-Hall do Brasil, Ltda., *Rio de Janeiro*

Contents

PART 1   INTRODUCTION

PART 2   PLANNING

PART 3   ORGANIZING

PART 4   LEADING

PART 5   CONTROLLING

INTRODUCTION

Welcome to Stephen P. Robbins' and David A. De Cenzo's *Fundamentals of Management*! The text and supplementary materials have been designed to provide you, the instructor, with the most up-to-date and easy-to-use information on the market. The principles of management course for which this book is designed is one of the most enjoyable and challenging courses to teach. It is enjoyable because of the wide variety of topics explored throughout the course. Students find general management topics interesting, exciting, and contemporary. Issues involved in planning, organizing, leading, and controlling are challenging. Unfortunately, because of the breadth of the subject matter, it is not possible to do much more than skim over the surface in order to provide students with the vital information that they will need to know about managers and management.

In this *Instructor's Resource Manual*, I have attempted to provide you with the type of information that instructors find useful in teaching courses on basic management. Each of the textbook's 16 chapters has been outlined and expanded upon so that you will have a solid and comprehensive reference source to use in conjunction with the other supplements. I am confident that you will enjoy using the book and all the associated materials!

There are some people I would like to recognize for their assistance in this project. The first, of course, is Lisamarie Brassini, for offering me the opportunity to participate in the endeavor. Credit is also due Mary Coulter, for her substantial effort in writing the *Instructor's Resource Manual* for the fourth edition of Robbins' *Management*.

Tara Radin
Darden School of Business Administration, University of Virginia

CONTENTS

OF

MANUAL

This *Instructor's Resource Manual* is designed to be used as a self-contained package. Each section includes all of the material pertinent to the corresponding chapter in the book. Each chapter in the manual includes the following:

☞   **Lecture Outline**: This outline is a brief summary of the chapter material and includes references to page numbers to help you plan lectures around specific material. Having the page numbers accessible allows you to make reading assignments without having to thumb through the book.

☞   **Annotated Outline**: This is the comprehensive outline of the chapter material. It includes page references for the major chapter headings. Additional spacing is provided so you can make personal notations about material you want to make sure to cover in class. Most of the chapter definitions are noted within this outline for your convenience as well. In addition, it is separated from the other material so you can remove the pages and use them in class as lecture notes.

☞   **Answers to Review and Discussion Questions**: This section includes thorough answers to all of the questions posed at the end of each chapter. Some of these questions are primarily factual in nature and directly assess students' understanding of the chapters' contents. These questions can also be used to provoke in-class discussions or as exam questions. Other questions are primarily applications-oriented questions that help to assess students' abilities to use the concepts discussed in the chapter. Many of these are also thought-provoking questions that ask students to examine how they would approach managerial situations and why.

☞ *Suggestions for Discussing Boxed Material*: Throughout the chapters, the authors have inserted "boxed in" material that expands upon what is in the text. I have provided comments and questions pertaining to the "boxed in" material that you can use to get students talking about this material.

☞ *Discussion of Self-Assessment Exercises*: This is one of the more unique features of the textbook, for, in every chapter, it affords students the opportunity to assess their skills, abilities, and thoughts as they relate to the chapter material. In this part, I offer suggestions for how you can tie the exercises into classroom discussions and guide students' further thoughts.

☞ *Discussion of Class Exercise*: The Class Exercises ask students to explore their managerial thoughts and abilities personally and compare them with their peers. These exercises are also aimed at teaching students to work in teams, an increasingly important ability. I offer suggestions as to how you can approach the exercises and incorporate them in class discussions.

☞ *Answers to Case Application Questions*: The case applications describe organizations and the situations that managers face. I provide answers to the questions that follow the cases.

☞ *Discussion of Video Cases*: The Video Cases comprise an important component of the educational supplements provided with the textbook. They come from the *Prentice Hall/ABC News Video Library* and include clips from current ABC programs. Each of the video cases has been selected to illustrate the concepts being covered in the chapter material. I expect that you and your students will find these clips intriguing and educational. I have provided a short synopsis of the videos and suggestions for how you can incorporate them in class discussions. In addition, I have provided answers to the questions presented at the end of the cases. Look for an additional exercise called "Project Video" in the Applications Pack supplement that you can assign your students to complete on the video cases.

SAMPLE SYLLABI

Course Description

This is an introductory course in management theory in practice that is designed to cover the fundamentals. Management is presented as a discipline and as a process. Major topic areas will include the scope and evolution of management, decision making, organizing, leading, and controlling.

Required Text

Robbins, Stephen P. and De Cenzo, David A., *Fundamentals of Management* (New Jersey: Prentice-Hall, 1994).

Objectives of the Course

1. To acquaint students with the management process. This includes understanding the theory behind and the practical applications of management.

2. To assist students in developing personal philosophies of management.

Assignments

1. *Readings*: Students are expected to complete the reading assignments by the date noted on the class outline.

2. *Exercises/Cases*: Students will be assigned to a series of exercises/cases to be worked on individually and in groups throughout the semester. These exercises provide practical application of management tools. These are considered an essential component of your learning about management.

3. *Tests*: Two exams will be given, one midterm and one final examination.

Class Outline (11 weeks)

Week	Topics	Assignment
1	Introduction: Managers and Management Changing Face of Management	1, 2
2	Foundations of Planning Planning Tools and Techniques	3, 4
3	Foundations of Decision Making	5
4	Foundations of Organizing Organization Design for the Twenty-first Century	6, 7
5	Human Resource Management Managing Change and Innovation	8, 9
6	MIDTERM	
7	Foundations of Behavior Understanding Groups and Teams	10, 11
8	Motivating Employees Leadership and Supervision	12, 13
9	Communication and Conflict Management	14
10	Foundations of Controlling Control Tools and Techniques	15, 16
11	FINAL EXAM	

Class Outline (16 weeks)

Week	Topics	Assignment
1	Introduction: Managers and Management Changing Face of Management	1, 2
2	Foundations of Planning	3
3	Planning Tools and Techniques	4
4	Foundations of Decision Making	5
5	Foundations of Organizing	6
6	Organization Design for the Twenty-first Century	7
7	Human Resource Management	8
8	Managing Change and Innovation	9
9	MIDTERM	
10	Foundations of Behavior	10
11	Understanding Groups and Teams	11
12	Motivating Employees	12
13	Leadership and Supervision	13
14	Communication and Conflict Management	14
15	Foundations of Controlling Control Tools and Techniques	15, 16
16	FINAL EXAM	

$\mathcal{P}$art 1

CHAPTER 1   MANAGERS AND MANAGEMENT

✓ LECTURE OUTLINE

✓ Annotated Outline

I. **INTRODUCTION** — p. 2

This chapter introduces the concept of management and managers. Its focus is on addressing four questions:

A. *Who* **are managers?**

Notes:

_____
_____
_____
_____

B. *What* **is management?**

Notes:

_____
_____
_____
_____

C. *What* **do managers do?**

Notes:

_____
_____
_____
_____

D. *Why* **should we study management?**

Notes:

_____
_____
_____
_____

II. **WHO ARE MANAGERS AND WHERE DO THEY WORK?** — p. 2

Managers work in organizations and direct the activities of others.

A. **Common characteristics of all organizations**

Organizations have distinct purposes or goals and are made up of people. They operate within systematic structures through which authority is assigned.

Notes:

_____

_____

_____

_____

B. **Managers vs. operatives employees**

Managers oversee the work of others while operatives focus only on the work assigned to them.

Notes:

_____

_____

_____

_____

C. **Classification of managers**

Managers are referred to according to their levels of responsibility. At the lowest level are the *first-line managers*, often called supervisors, who are responsible for the day-to-day work of the operative employees. The *middle managers* are at the next level and they are responsible for turning the general goals articulated by top management into specific work that lower level managers can perform. *Top management* often includes officers such as the managing director, vice president, and president, who establish the direction of the organization.

Notes:

_____

_____

_____

_____

III. **WHAT IS MANAGEMENT AND WHAT DO MANAGERS DO?** — 4

There are common characteristics to managers' jobs. We can begin to understand what these characteristics are by using different approaches to understanding what management is and what managers do.

A. **Defining management**

Management is the process of getting activities done efficiently with and through other people.

1. The *process* includes the functions or primary activities performed by managers.

2. *Efficiency* refers to the relationship between inputs and outputs and refers to efforts to minimize resource costs.

3. *Effectiveness* refers to goal attainment.

4. Managers seek to be both efficient and effective.

Notes:

_____

_____

_____

_____

B. **Four functions of management**

Henri Fayol, a French industrialist from the early part of the 1900s, proposed that managers perform five management functions: POCCC (plan, organize, command, coordinate, control). These functions still provide the basis around which popular management textbooks are organized. The functions have been condensed into four.

1. *Planning* includes defining goals, establishing strategy, and developing plans to coordinate activities.

2. *Organizing* is determining what tasks are to be done, who is to do them, how the tasks are to be grouped, who reports to whom, and where decisions are to be made.

3. *Leading* includes motivating subordinates, directing others, selecting the most effective communication channels, and resolving conflicts.

4. *Controlling* is monitoring activities to ensure that they are being accomplished as planned and correcting any significant deviations.

Although the functional approach is clear and simple, critics have suggested that it does not provide an accurate description of what managers actually do.

C. Management roles

In the late 1960s Henry Mintzberg conducted a precise study of managers at work. His findings challenged several long-held beliefs about the manager's job. He concluded that managers perform ten different, but highly interrelated roles. *Management roles* refers to specific categories of managerial behavior.

Notes:

_____

_____

_____

_____

D. Evidence of roles in managers' jobs

The type of roles that managers perform tend to fall into three general categories.

1. *Interpersonal roles* included figurehead, leadership, and liaison activities.

2. *Informational roles* included monitoring, disseminating, and spokesperson activities.

3. *Decisional roles* included those of entrepreneur, disturbance handler, resource allocator, and negotiator.

Notes:

_____

_____

_____

_____

E. Are effective managers also successful managers?

A study by Fred Luthans and his associates found that managers who were most effective in their jobs were not necessarily the ones promoted the fastest.

1. Managers engaged in four managerial activities.

a. *Traditional management*, including decision making, planning, and controlling.

b. *Communication*, including exchanging routine information and processing paperwork.

c. *Human resource management*, including motivating, disciplining, managing conflict, staffing, and training.

d. *Networking*, including socializing, politicking, and interacting with outsiders.

2. "Effective" managers and "successful" managers emphasized these activities differently.

Notes:

_____
_____
_____
_____
_____

F. Is the manager's job universal?

1. All managers perform essentially the same functions, but lower-level managers emphasize leading while upper-level managers spend more of their time planning, organizing, and controlling.

2. Certain skills are generally considered important to managers. During the 1970s, management researcher Robert L. Katz found that managers must possess four types of skills: conceptual, human, technical, and political skills.

Notes:

_____
_____
_____
_____

G. Managing in profit and not-for-profit organizations

For the most part, the manager's job is the same in both profit and not-for-profit organizations. There are certain commonalities to managers' jobs, regardless of the differences between the types of organizations where they work.

Notes:

_____

_____

_____

_____

H. **Managing in small and large organizations**

Managers in small businesses tend to emphasize the spokesperson role and are generalists. Also, the formal structure and nature of a manager's job in a large organization is replaced by more informality in a small firm.

Notes:

_____

_____

_____

_____

I. **Transferability of management concepts across national borders**

When managers work in different countries, they often need to modify their practices.

Notes:

_____

_____

_____

_____

IV. **HOW MUCH IMPORTANCE DOES THE MARKETPLACE PUT ON MANAGERS?** — p. 14

Managers earn more than operatives because their decisions have a significant effect on the organization's performance and because of the inadequate supply of effective managers.

A. **Do all managers make six-figure incomes?**

Six-figure salaries tend to be reserved for senior executives. A manager's salary tends to depend on numerous variables, such as education, experience, ability, type of business, and comparable community and industry pay standards.

Notes:

_____

_____

_____

_____

V.   WHY STUDY MANAGEMENT? — p. 16

Management is important in our society today. Accordingly, there are two reasons for studying management.

A.   We interact with organizations every day of our lives. Every product we use and every action we take is provided or affected by organizations. These organizations require managers.

Notes:

_____

_____

_____

_____

B.   Upon graduating, you will either manage or be managed. A course in management provides insights into the workings of organizations.

Notes:

_____

_____

_____

_____

VI.   HOW DO WE STUDY MANAGEMENT? — p. 17

Although many approaches to management were proposed through the mid-1900s, recent years have witnessed their consolidation into three integrated approaches.

A.   **The process approach**

The *process approach* describes how management performs the functions of planning, organizing, leading, and controlling. An article by Professor Harold Koontz on the "management theory jungle" proposed that each approach had something to offer management theory. A process approach was nevertheless needed to encompass and synthesize the diversity.

Notes:

_____

_____

_____

_____

B. **How can a systems approach integrate management concepts?**

The *systems approach* is a theory that sees an organization as a set of interrelated and interdependent parts.

1. There are two basic types of systems.

   a. Closed systems are not influenced by and do not interact with their environment.

   b. Open systems are dynamic systems that interact with and respond to their environment.

2. Systems-perspective advocates envision the organization as being made up of interdependent factors. The manager's job is to ensure that all parts of the system are coordinated internally so that the organization's goals can be reached.

3. The I - T - O (input, transformation, output) model is often used as a graphical illustration of an organization as an open system.

Notes:

_____

_____

_____

_____

C. **A "contingency approach" to management**

The *contingency approach* involves recognizing and responding to situational variables as they arise. It has been used in recent years to replace simplistic principles of management and to integrate much of management theory.

Notes:

_____

_____

_____

_____

✓ Answers to Review and Discussion Questions

1. *What is an organization? Why are managers important to an organization's success?*

   An organization is a systematic arrangement of people to accomplish some specific purpose. Managers are important to an organization's success because they direct and coordinate activities so the organization can reach its goals.

2. *Are all effective organizations also efficient? Discuss.*

   All effective organizations are not necessarily efficient. Effectiveness is concerned with goal attainment while efficiency is concerned with resource usage. An organization can achieve its goals, but do so by being wasteful and using an inordinate amount of input resources.

3. *What four common functions do all managers perform? Briefly describe them.*

   All managers should perform the functions of planning, organizing, leading, and controlling. Planning includes plans to coordinate activities. Organizing determines what tasks are to be done, who is to do them, how the tasks are to be grouped, who reports to whom, and where decisions are to be made. Leading includes motivating subordinates, directing others, selecting the most effective communication channels, and resolving conflicts. Controlling insures that activities are accomplished as planned and any significant deviations are corrected.

4. *Contrast the four functions with Mintzberg's ten roles.*

   Mintzberg has defined ten roles of managers categorized into interpersonal, informational, and decisional roles. While these roles are more specific descriptions of managers, they reconcile with the four managerial functions of planning, organizing, leading, and controlling. The similarities are overlapping, yet the differences are based on intermixing management activities. There is also the possibility that Mintzberg's roles may only be applicable to top management positions.

5. *What are the four managerial activities identified by Luthans? Contrast the emphasis placed on these four activities by average, successful, and effective managers.*

Luthans and his associates found that managers engaged in traditional management activities, communication, human resource management, and networking. The average manager spent most of his or her time in traditional management activities and communicating. The successful manager spent nearly half of his or her time networking. The effective manager emphasized communication.

6. *How does a manger's job change with his or her level in the organization?*

The job of manager changes only in degrees as one moves up in the organization. All managers plan, organize, lead, and control. Yet higher level managers tend to plan more while lower level managers tend to lead more.

7. *Is your college instructor a manager? Discuss in terms of both Fayol's managerial functions and Mintzberg's managerial roles.*

A college instructor would generally not fall within the definition of a manager when utilizing Fayol's managerial functions. This is predominantly due to the relationship between instructors and students. Students are not employees, but more appropriately, clients. In fact, in some unusual cases, an instructor may have little say about the course content or how it is to be taught. In these instances, the instructor clearly makes few decisions. Regardless, college instructors, in their position as teacher (in contrast to that of, say department head) are not managers.

In terms of Mintzberg's managerial roles, college instructors perhaps are involved in some ways in the interpersonal, informational, and decisional roles. For example, a college instructor could be seen as a liaison (interpersonal role), a monitor and disseminator (both informational roles), and a disturbance handler and negotiator (both decisional roles).

8. *In what ways would the mayor's job in a large city and the president's job in a large corporation be similar? In what ways would they be different?*

Both the mayor and corporate president oversee an organization. Both plan, organize, lead, and control. Both seek effectiveness through efficiency. The major difference is that the mayor's organization has a more ambiguous definition of effectiveness since it has no "bottom line." It is more difficult, therefore, to judge the effectiveness of the mayor than the corporate president.

9. *Some so-called managers oversee only assembly line robots or a roomful of computers. Can they really be managers if they have no subordinates?*

Using the definition from the text chapter, managers must direct the activities of others. In practice, there are individuals who do not have subordinates but are labelled managers. Again, for our definitional purposes, a manager must direct other persons.

10. *How might the job of an owner-manager of a small business compare with the job of president of a large corporation?*

The small business manager's job is more of a generalist. His or her job will combine the activities of a large corporation's CEO with many of the day-to-day activities undertaken by a first-line supervisor. Additionally, the structure and formality that characterize a manager's job in a large corporation tend to give way to informality in small, owner-managed firms.

11. *How is the process approach integrative?*

The process approach is integrative because it encompasses and synthesizes the diverse schools of management thought. All managers should perform planning, organizing, leading, and controlling activities continuously. Scientific management contributions, the general administrative theorists, human resources advocates, and quantitative theorists all can be subsumed under one or more of the functions in the process approach.

12. *Explain how practicing managers can benefit by using the contingency approach.*

Because organizations differ in size, objectives, tasks to be performed, and environmental uncertainty, a general theory of management applicable to all situations would be impossible. The contingency approach allows the manager to adapt his or her action to the situation and in so doing, increases the probability that the action will improve organizational effectiveness.

✔ SUGGESTIONS FOR DISCUSSING BOXED MATERIAL

Mintzberg's Roles: You can use this material to encourage students to think critically about Mintzberg's role categories. Ask students to discuss what evidence there is that the categories are or are not applicable today.

Peter Lewis at Progressive Auto Insurance: This example helps to foster discussion about how managers can make a difference. How can you determine if a manager makes a difference? What if it's not possible to link his or her efforts to financial results?

✓ SUGGESTIONS FOR THE SELF-ASSESSMENT EXERCISE

This self assessment focuses on one's ability to manage. After answering and scoring, students should be divided into three groups: high scores (80-100); middle range scores (60-80); and low scores (below 60). Have each group respond to the following questions:

* Why do you think you have the skills to manage? Explain.

* How can you use this information in helping you to plan your career?

* How do you feel about/react to the other groups?

Emphasis should be placed here in recognizing that not all people have the ability or desire to manage and that's perfectly acceptable. Emphasize that what is *best* for you is what is *right* for you. Spend time on recognizing the benefit of the need for managers and operatives within organizations. This is one way to begin to reduce the "we-they" syndrome between management and operatives.

✓ COMMENTS ON CLASS EXERCISE

There are several ways you can encourage discussion:

* Encourage students to think about the managers they know, directly or indirectly, before they start answering the questions. What makes managers successful or unsuccessful?

* Mention that not everyone wants to be a manager. There is not anything wrong with not wanting to be a manager. Students who do not aim at becoming managers might want to think about why they do not want to be managers. They also should think about what they still gain by learning about managers.

* You might want to take the class outside for this exercise, or assign it as homework, to give students time to think about the questions and talk to each other in a casual setting without time constraints. This might enable students to launch into interesting conversations that they could then bring back to the classroom.

✔ ANSWERS TO CASE APPLICATION QUESTIONS

1. *One of the more difficult situations a new supervisor will face is interacting with former operative colleagues. As such, once someone becomes a member of management, do you think they stop socializing (e.g. having lunch, going to parties, etc.) with those who are not in supervisory positions? Why or why not?*

   Moving up in a company does not mean that you have to lose touch with former operative colleagues. The nature of your relationship will likely change, though, as it would if you had moved to a different city, department, or company. Your priorities change and you no longer have all the same things in common. If all you initially had in common was the operative work that you did, then it is likely that you will stop socializing, unless you can find new common areas of interest, such as sports or hobbies. If you and your former operative colleagues already shared outside interests, there is no reason for you to stop enjoying them together.

   In Mr. Dalton's situation, it appears that he and his "friends"—at least as a group—shared little in common other than their dislike of management. Unless they find other common interests, it is unlikely that they will ask him to "do lunch" again, or that he will accept such an invitation.

2. *If you were Charles Dalton, how would you react to your former colleagues who have now placed you on the "bash" list?*

   Mr. Dalton must recognize that the situation has changed. He now has more in common with supervisors than with his former operative colleagues. It is not likely that he could say anything to change their behavior, because he now belongs to the general category of people that they enjoy ridiculing. He should politely ignore negative references to his supervisory role and look for other areas of common interest, if they exist. If they choose to remain in touch socially, they should perhaps avoid discussing work.

3. *Interview someone in a sales manager position. Have them compare their job roles and functions with someone who is a salesperson. How closely did their roles and functions compare with those discussed in the text?*

Initially, you should be prepared to allow or not allow students to interview their parents who are or have been sales managers. You might want to suggest that students find the manager where they shop for hardware, clothes, gifts, or groceries—Lowe's, Macy's, Pier 1, or Fresh Fields, for example. You might want to recommend that they first ask the sales managers how long they have worked at the company and look for someone with at least a year of experience at the company.

Expect any number of issues to emerge out of the interviews. Some might lead to a discussion of promotion from within versus hiring from the outside, management/subordinate relations, job satisfaction, job enrichment, and empowerment.

You may want to suggest that students ask the sales managers they interview a few extra questions. How could management/subordinate relations be made more friendly? How could management help salespeople enjoy their jobs more? Is it the positions or the people in the positions that lead to the level of job satisfaction and the nature of management/subordinate relations?

✓ SUGGESTIONS FOR USING VIDEO CASE

"Kay Graham of the Washington Post"

Running Time: 5:21

This video case provides a good example of a dynamic and energetic female manager. Kay Graham managed the Washington Post from 1963-1991 when she stepped down as chief executive officer. During those 28 years, her determination to set high standards of excellence helped to turn the newspaper into the successful and powerful institution that it is today.

Use this video case as either an introduction or a conclusion to the chapter. As an introduction to the chapter, emphasize the inexperience and lack of training that Ms. Graham had and yet overcame by listening and by hiring top-notch employees. As a conclusion to the chapter, ask students to note examples of managerial functions and/or managerial roles that Ms. Graham exhibits.

ANSWERS TO QUESTIONS

1. *What factors, if any, in Ms. Graham's background might suggest success as a manager? What does this suggest for using personality-type to predict management success?*

   Upon looking at Ms. Graham's background and the description of her as "shy and unassuming," it is hard to believe that she became the successful manager of the Post that she did. However, she knew how to listen and she knew how to learn. These skills served her well as she took over the responsibilities of running the Post.

   The fact that Ms. Graham saw herself as shy and unassuming and yet was able to effectively manage a large and successful organization shows that you cannot always predict management success by looking at personality.

2. *Kay Graham illustrates that you don't need to study management to be an effective manager. Discuss the advantages of management education over "on-the-job" learning.*

   Although you may not need to study management to be an effective manager, a management education can provide one with information about organizations and different approaches to managing. Managing different types and sizes of organizations may require different skills and activities, yet management is still universal in all organizations. By studying management, you can be aware of these differences and perhaps not spend time "reinventing the wheel."

3. ***Graham says, "Organizations need young people." But don't they also need experience? Discuss.***

Yes, organizations need both. The experience and wisdom of mature managers and the enthusiasm and flexibility of young managers can provide the basis for effective and efficient management of organizations.

CHAPTER 2   THE CHANGING FACE OF MANAGEMENT

✓ LECTURE OUTLINE

✓ ANNOTATED OUTLINE

I.   **INTRODUCTION** — p. 26

The current dynamic business environment is causing managers to rethink traditional business practices. To enable their organizations to succeed today, managers are becoming fast, and flexible. They are also increasing quality, teamwork, and attention to ethics, and decreasing hierarchy and bureaucracy. A number of trends are thus changing the way managers do their jobs.

Notes:

_____

_____

_____

_____

II. **THE INCREASINGLY DYNAMIC ENVIRONMENT** — p. 27

One of the greatest challenges confronted by today's managers is figuring out how to let go of the past. To succeed, organizations have to learn new ways to deal with the international market, involve a more diverse work force, decrease bureaucracy, and increase creativity.

A.   **What is the Environment?**

The impact of the external environment on manager's actions and behaviors cannot be overemphasized. There are forces in the environment that play a major role in shaping managers' endeavors.

1.   The *environment* is defined as outside institutions or forces that potentially affect an organization's performance.

2.   The *general environment* includes everything outside the organization.

3.   The *specific environment* is the part of the environment that is directly relevant to the achievement of an organization's goals.

4.   Organizations depend upon different environmental factors.

_____

_____

_____

_____

B. **Is there a Global Village?**

Managers are moving beyond national borders and learning to adapt to unfamiliar cultures, systems, and techniques as the world becomes a *global village*.

1. Although international businesses have been around at least since the time of Christopher Columbus, *multinational corporations* (*MNCs*) really didn't become popular until the mid-1960s. Multinational corporations are based in a single home country from which they manage significant simultaneous operations in two or more countries.

2. *Transnational corporations* (*TNCs*) maintain significant operations in more than one country simultaneously, but allow decision making to take place at the local level, often by nationals hired to run domestic operations in each country.

3. A company's national origin is no longer a very good measure of where it does business or of the national origin of the employees.

4. *Regional trading alliances*, such as the 12-nation European Community (EC) and the North American Free-Trade Agreement (NAFTA) are reshaping global competition by removing trade barriers such as tariffs to stimulate trade among members.

5. The fall of communism during the last several years has created many openings for free markets and profit-seeking enterprises.

6. Eastern European countries are becoming a source of well-trained, reliable, low-cost labor.

7. As international business increases, managers are recognizing the importance of the old adage, "When in Rome, do as the Romans do."

8. Geert Hofstede's framework, which indicates that national culture plays a significant role in defining employees' work-related values and attitudes, is useful for gaining insight into working in the global village.

Notes:

_____

_____

_____

_____

C. **Why are the Big Guys Laying Off?**

Many organizations are downsizing to gain flexibility in responding to the rapidly changing business environment. Some large organizations are able to balance large size and agility, but most are attempting to eliminate layers of institutional bureaucracy.

Notes:

_____

_____

_____

_____

D. **Why is the Future of Business with Small Business**

Big businesses are attempting to model their operations after those of small businesses because small businesses are able to get closer to the customer and to respond more quickly to change.

1. People who tend to work independently, take calculated risks, and accept the making of mistakes are oftentimes referred to as *entrepreneurs*.

2. When organizations encourage internal entrepreneurial activity it is called *intrapreneurship*.

Notes:

_____

_____

_____

_____

E. **What is the Work Force of 2001 Going to Look Like?**

The work force of 2001 is going to be much more diverse. *Work force diversity* refers to employees in organizations that are heterogeneous in terms of gender, race, ethnicity or other characteristics. The challenge for managers is to make organizations more accommodating to diverse groups of people by addressing different lifestyles, family needs, and work styles.

Notes:

_____

_____

_____

_____

F. **Why the Increased Concern with Quality?**

Total quality management is a philosophy of management that is driven by customer needs and expectations.

1. TQM was inspired by a small group of quality experts, chief among them an American named W. Edwards Deming.

2. TQM represents a counterpoint to earlier management theorists who believed that low costs were the only road to increased productivity.

3. The objective of TQM is to create an organization committed to continuous improvement.

4. Attention to TQM and continuous improvement is becoming a requirement for organizations who want to remain competitive.

Notes:

_____

_____

_____

_____

G. **What Responsibility, if any, do Managers have to the Larger Society?**

Since the 1960s, managers have begun wrestling with the degree to which they should consider the social ramifications of their business decisions. There are two opposing positions regarding social responsibility.

1. The classical view is the view that management's only social responsibility is to maximize profits. Economist Milton Friedman is the most outspoken advocate of this view.

2. The socioeconomic view is the view that management's social responsibility goes well beyond the making of profits to include protecting and improving society's welfare.

Notes:

_____

_____

_____

_____

H. **How can an Organization go from Obligations to Responsiveness?**

Three different levels of social involvement can be defined.

1. *Social responsibility* is defined as an obligation beyond that required by law and economics for a firm to pursue long-term goals that are good for society.

2. *Social obligation* defines the obligation of a business to meet its economic and legal responsibilities.

3. *Social responsiveness* is the capacity of a firm to adapt to changing societal conditions.

Notes:

_____

_____

_____

_____

I. **How is Social Responsibility Extended to Women in the Workplace?**

During the past several years, managers have become increasingly concerned about their treatment of women, particularly with the protection of women from *sexual harassment* in the workplace. Sexual harassment is behavior marked by sexually suggestive remarks, unwanted touching and sexual advances, requests for sexual favors, or other verbal or physical conduct of a sexual nature. Organizations must establish and reinforce clear and strong policies against such behavior to avoid liability.

Notes:

_____

_____

_____

_____

J. **Why must Managers Think in Terms of Quantum Changes Rather than Incremental Change?**

The process of continuous improvement creates a false sense of security in that it causes managers to feel as if they are ttaking progressive action when it could be that they are merely avoiding what the organization really needs: radical or quantum change, known as *re-engineering*. TQM is thus not always the appropriate first step.

Notes:

_____

_____

_____

_____

III. **NEW CHALLENGES FOR MANAGERS** — p. 44

Managers, along with organizations, must change with the times.

A. **How do Managers Turn from Bosses into Coaches?**

1. Managers are finding that they can increase productivity and quality by motivating and coaching employees, instead of merely by assigning more tasks.

2. *Empowerment* is increasing the decision-making discretion of workers. It builds on ideas originally expounded by the human resources theorists.

3. The need for quick, knowledgeable decision making and the reality that downsizing has decreased the availability of middle-managers support the move toward empowerment.

4. Business managers are beginning to emulate sports coaches in their leadership of work teams.

Notes:

_____

_____

_____

_____

B. **How do Manager's Motivate Today's Workers?**

In deciding how to motivate employees, managers must recognize that there is a **bi-modal workforce**. This refers to the fact that employees tend to perform either low-skilled service jobs for near-minimum wage or high-skilled, well-paying jobs.

Notes:

_____

_____

_____

_____

C. **How do You Improve their Ethics?**

Ethics and the perceived decline in ethical standards are receiving much attention.

1. Behaviors that were once considered disgraceful have unfortunately become, to many businesspeople, acceptable or necessary business practices.

2. Ethics refers to the rules and principles that define right and wrong conduct. There are ethical dimensions to managerial decisions.

3. Various factors influence whether a manager acts ethically or unethically, including morality, individual differences, organizational culture, and the issue being called into question.

4. *Codes of ethics* can be used to increase ethical behavior. They are formal statements of organizations' primary values and the ethical rules they expect employees to follow.

Notes:

_____

_____

_____

_____

D. **What's More Important: Stability or Flexibility?**

Change today takes place at an unprecedented rate and forces companies to become flexible to remain competitive.

Notes:

_____

_____

_____

_____

E. **How do we make People in Organizations More Sensitive to Cultural Diversity?**

Many organizations are implementing training programs designed to raise diversity consciousness among employees.

Notes:

_____

_____

_____

_____

✓ ANSWERS TO REVIEW AND DISCUSSION QUESTIONS

1. *Why must managers pay attention to the global village?*

   With the globalization of the business world, managers cannot afford to ignore the global village. Even organizations who are not actively moving abroad must pay attention to the foreigners moving in. The global economy creates opportunities by opening up huge markets. Large markets can translate into increased sales and lower costs (through economies of scale). However, a global economy also creates the threat of new competitors, many with competitive advantages that a firm operating in a national market doesn't have. Oftentimes, organizations feel they must move in before a new competitor emerges or an old one becomes stronger.

2. *What is the difference between a multinational corporation and a transnational corporations?*

   Both types of corporations have significant operations in two or more countries. A multinational corporations maintains decision making in the home country where it is based, whereas a transnational corporation allows for decision making to take place locally, typically by nationals hired to run domestic operations.

3. *"Corporate downsizing for better customer service and more efficiency was just a ruse by large companies to reduce their payrolls and increase their profits." Do you agree or disagree with the statement? Explain?*

   Disagree. While it is probably true that there are organizations who are downsizing for short-term profits, most organizations are looking toward the long term in their efforts. They recognize that the competitive companies of the 1990s are lean and perform the maximum amount of work with the minimum number of workers. At the same time, these companies are taking steps to empower employees and keep morale up. The overwhelming success of the leaner companies indicates that planned downsizing is more than a tool for payroll reduction.

4. *Given that all different kinds of people will comprise tomorrow's organizations, what managerial implications will this diversity bring about?*

   Increased workforce diversity is going to require enhanced external recruitment efforts and internal sensitivity training. It will also require more flexible scheduling and improved facilities, for people such as working parents and the handicapped.

5. *"TQM includes contributions from scientific management, the human resource approach, and the quantitative approach." Do you agree or disagree? Discuss.*

Agree. TQM focuses on customers, continual improvement, quality of everything the organization does, accurate measurement, and empowerment of employees. Each of these areas can be seen as important components of the scientific management approach or the human resource approach or the quantitative approach.

6. *In what ways do you think the changing face of management has changed or will change the way in which a company selects and trains managers?*

The changing face of management is likely to cause organizations to have to alter selection processes to look for flexible people who pay attention to ethics and the environment, and are interested in quality and creativity. In addition, the organizations are no longer looking for life-time employees. Training will similarly have to be revamped to emphasize diversity, ethics, and quality. In addition, with change becoming a constant, so must training.

7. *"Coaching will never replace traditional managers. There's too much at stake to be left up to coaching techniques." Do you agree or disagree with the statement? Explain.*

Disagree. While coaching may not work as successfully in some types of organizations, in many it has already taken hold, if, for no other reason, by necessity. Downsizing has drastically reduced the number of middle managers so that lower level employees have been forced to take on more responsibilities. In many cases, coaching has also become preferable to traditional managers because it transfers decision making to the people closest to the situation—those in the best position to make decisions—and leaves the supervisor free to take care of the exceptions.

8. *Would you prefer to work in a company that has a good salary, but no reward for your performance, or one in which your base salary is lower, but you have an opportunity to more than double your yearly earnings based on your performance? Discuss.*

Traditional workers would often prefer the stable salary. Entrepreneurial workers tend to prefer performance-based pay. Such compensation works well for both the organization and the ambitious employee because productivity and pay increase. Employees with a stake in the outcome tend to work more productively than those who do not have such a stake.

9. *Over the past 20 years, has business become less willing to accept its societal responsibility? Explain.*

   Business has not been less willing to accept its social responsibilities. However, the changes in societal expectations have occurred faster than business has been able to adapt.

10. *While Playboy Enterprises has a woman president, the magazine it publishes contains photographs and stories that may be regarded as exploitive. With this in mind, discuss the following: "Companies that promote women are acting unethically." Could Playboy be both?*

    The ethical issues that are involved here include conflicts between organizational and social values and exploitation of certain groups. Playboy Enterprises would probably be the first to argue that they are not exploiting women but rather glorifying the female gender. The fact that Playboy Enterprises has a woman president illustrates the company does not totally demean women.

✓ SUGGESTIONS FOR DISCUSSING BOXED MATERIAL

Hofstede's Cultural Variables: Use this material to foster a discussion about how people differ around the country, as well as around the world. Ask students to comment about any reactions they might have had during their travels.

Pam Del Duca, President and CEO, DELSTAR Group: Ask students what sort of social responsibility efforts they have witnessed. Were DELSTAR's actions appropriate? Would they encourage their companies to engage in social responsibility? What ideas do they have?

Guidelines to Protect a Company from Sexual Harassment Charges: This material can foster an engaging conversation about what responsibilities organizations have toward their employees. This is a question that can be posed to the students. Also, are these guidelines adequate? Are they excessive? Do students have other ideas? Who can be victims of sexual harassment? Make sure they acknowledge that both men and women can be victims. In addition, perhaps asks students how they would discourage sexual harassment in their organizations.

✓ SUGGESTIONS FOR THE SELF-ASSESSMENT EXERCISE

We know from the chapter that values are basic convictions about what is right and wrong. This self-assessment exercise focuses on personal value preferences. Have students answer and score the exercise. Because of the personal and individual nature of this exercise, I would suggest dividing students into pairs to discuss the implications of their results. Have each pair of students answer the following questions:

* Why did I choose the one that I did as *greatest importance to me*?

* Why did I choose the one that I did as *least important to me*?

* What does this assessment tell me about myself?

* What implications do these values have for me as a manager?

* Do you think your values would be different 5 years from now? 20 years from now? Why?

✓ COMMENTS ON CLASS EXERCISE

This exercise is designed to show students how **much**, or how **little** they know about international culture. Have students do the self-assessment and self-scoring. Then ask how many got all 10 right, 9 right, 8 right, and so on. Then ask students the following questions to generate class discussion:

* Why do you think you know so little (or much, if student responses turn out that way!) about international culture?

* What can you do *as a student* to learn more about the customs, practices, and facts regarding different countries?

* What do you think organizations can do to better prepare managers for dealing with different cultures in different countries?

✓ Answers to Case Application Questions

1. *How can ISO 9000 help an organization with meeting global village demands? With producing quality products?*

   An ISO rating for a company's products and services can serve as an international competitive advantage because it can give the company access to a wider customer base. Just as companies are paying attention to quality so are customers, and the ISO rating gives customers around the world a way to measure the quality they are buying. In addition, because the requirements of the ISO 9000 are so stringent, even if a company does not earn such a rating, the improvements made toward that end are likely to nevertheless enable the company to produce higher quality products.

2. *Are ISO 9000 and re-engineering synonymous? Discuss.*

   ISO 9000 and re-engineering are similar, though not synonymous. Re-engineering is the process that organizations go through to change processes and ISO 9000 is an international measurement of the quality of those processes that organizations aim for.

3. *Do the certifying and standardizing of management practices inherent in achieving ISO 9000 standards suggest that there is "one best way" to run a company? Discuss.*

   The popularity of the ISO rating does not mean that there is one best way to run a company. What it does mean, though, is that it is best for organizations to eliminate errors and improve quality. Organizations are free to increase productivity and quality however they choose. The ISO rating measures for the general presence of quality, not for specific process attributes.

✓ Suggestions for Using Video Case

"General Electric's Automatic Coffeemaker"

Running Time: 12:22

This video case provides a good example of the types of decisions that corporate executives face and the implications that their decisions can have on society. As the case first points out, it is important to try to understand what General Electric knew and when they knew it with respect to the malfunctioning coffeemaker.

The video would probably best be used after you have discussed the chapter. At this point, students will have been introduced to the concept of social obligations and ethical decision making. If they have not been through this material, students might see only one side to this issue, the consumer's, and not fully comprehend why General Electric took the position it did, although in retrospect the decisions were not conscientious ones.

Answers to Questions

1. *Was GE meeting its basic social obligation with its coffeemaker problem? Explain.*

    General Electric felt that it was meeting its basic social obligation. The company noted that only a small fraction of the 9 million coffeemakers in use were a problem. However, critics claim that the company knew it had a serious problem with the product and delayed taking any action.

2. *Why do you think GE's management ignored the danger associated with this product?*

    It is possible that GE's management assumed that the statistics were in its favor. After all, they put the probability at only 42 percent that no one would be hurt and that problems with the coffeemaker's design would result in only 168 claims. However, relying upon these statistics, GE's management ignored the fact that there was a 58 percent chance that someone would be hurt because of the product's design.

3. *Was GE's response consistent with a utilitarian view of ethics? Discuss.*

    GE's response would appear to be appropriate with a utilitarian view of ethics. In this approach, decisions are made solely on the basis of their outcomes or consequences.

Since executives at General Electric had determined that the percentage of coffeemakers with problems (hypothesized at 168 out of millions sold) would be infinitesimally small, they decided to proceed with production and marketing of the product. They perhaps believed that the outcomes even with a defective design flaw would be inconsequential.

4. *If GE is guilty of denying and covering up a defective product, should its management be punished? What do you think an appropriate punishment would be?*

If GE is guilty of denying and covering up a defective product, the managers responsible for making these decisions should be punished. If any laws or regulations were violated, such as those set forth by the Consumer Product Safety Commission, then managers should be convicted and punished for those offenses.

As far as an appropriate punishment, student responses could vary on this. More than likely, huge monetary fines and possible prison terms would be the probable punishment given by the courts.

Part 2

CHAPTER 3   FOUNDATIONS OF PLANNING

✓ LECTURE OUTLINE

ENTREPRENEURSHIP: A SPECIAL CASE OF STRATEGIC PLANNING? — p. 74

SUMMARY — p. 76

✓ ANNOTATED OUTLINE

I. **INTRODUCTION** — p. 56

Planning is one of the four functions of management. It plays an important role in the way managers do their jobs. The basics of planning are presented in this chapter.

Notes:

_____

_____

_____

_____

II. **PLANNING DEFINED** — p. 56

Planning involves defining the organization's objectives or goals, establishing an overall strategy for achieving those goals, and developing a comprehensive hierarchy of plans to integrate and coordinate activities. The term planning as used in this chapter refers to *formal* planning.

Notes:

_____

_____

_____

_____

III. **PURPOSE OF PLANNING** — p. 57

Planning is important and serves many significant purposes.

A. Planning gives direction to the organization.

B. Planning establishes coordinated effort.

C. Planning reduces uncertainty by anticipating change.

D. Planning clarifies the consequences of the actions managers might take.

E. Planning reduces overlapping and wasteful activities.

F. Planning establishes objectives or standards that facilitate control.

Notes:

_____
_____
_____
_____

IV. **PLANNING AND PERFORMANCE** — p. 58

Research has shown that we cannot assume organizations with formal planning processes *always* outperform those organizations that don't have formal planning processes.

A. Generally speaking, formal planning is associated with positive financial results.

Notes:

_____
_____
_____
_____

B. The *quality* of the planning process and appropriate *implementation* probably contribute more to high performance than does the *extent* of planning.

Notes:

_____
_____
_____
_____

C. When formal planning has been shown **not** to lead to higher performance, the environment is usually the reason.

_____

_____

_____

_____

V. TYPES OF PLANS — p. 59

Plans can be described by their *breadth*, *time frame*, and *specificity*.

A. Strategic planning vs. operational planning

Strategic plans are plans that are organization-wide, establish overall objectives, and position an organization in terms of its environment. *Operational plans* are plans that specify details on how overall objectives are to be achieved.

Notes:

_____

_____

_____

_____

B. The time frame for plans

Short-term plans are plans that cover less than one year. *Long-term plans* are plans that extend beyond five years.

Notes:

_____

_____

_____

_____

C. Specific plans vs. directional plans

Specific plans are plans that are clearly defined and leave no room for interpretation. *Directional plans* are flexible plans that set out general guidelines.

Notes:

_____
_____
_____
_____

VI.   **CONTINGENCY FACTORS AFFECTING PLANNING** — p. 60

Several contingency factors that affect planning can be identified.

A.   **Level in the organization**

Operational planning usually dominates the planning activities of lower-level managers. As managers are promoted through the levels of the organization, their planning becomes more strategic.

Notes:

_____
_____
_____
_____

B.   **The life cycle of the organization**

Organizations are known to go through a life cycle which is defined in terms of four stages: formation, growth, maturity, and decline. The length and specificity of plans should be adjusted at each stage.

Notes:

_____
_____
_____
_____

C.   **The degree of environmental uncertainty**

The greater the environmental uncertainty, the more plans should be directional and emphasis placed on the short term.

Notes:

_____

_____

_____

_____

D. **The length of future commitments**

The *commitment concept* says that plans should extend far enough to see through current commitments.

Notes:

_____

_____

_____

_____

VII. **MANAGEMENT BY OBJECTIVES** — p. 64

Management by objectives is a system that uses goals to motivate employees rather than control them. Managers and their subordinates set goals together. In addition, there are periodic reviews of progress toward the goals, and rewards are given according to the progress toward the goals.

A. **What is MBO?**

MBO is not a new concept. MBO makes objectives operational by devising a process by which they cascade down through the organization.

Notes:

_____

_____

_____

_____

B. **Common elements to an MBO program**

There are four ingredients common to MBO programs.

1. Goal specificity.

2. Participative decision making.

3. An explicit time period.

4. Performance feedback.

Notes:

_____

_____

_____

_____

VIII. THE IMPORTANCE OF AN ORGANIZATIONAL STRATEGY — p. 66

The environmental "shocks" of the 1970s and 1980s have forced managers into developing a systematic means of analyzing the environment and incorporating these findings into their organization. The use of strategic planning has become more prevalent in for-profit as well as in nonprofit organizations.

Notes:

_____

_____

_____

_____

IX. THE STRATEGIC MANAGEMENT PROCESS — p. 66

The strategic management process is a nine-step process encompassing strategic planning, implementation, and evaluation.

A. The operation of the strategic management process

1. **Step 1**

   Every organization has a *mission* that defines the purpose of the organization. It should answer the question of what business or businesses are we in.

Notes:

_____

_____

_____

_____

2. **Step 2**

Analyzing the environment is a critical step in the strategy process. A successful strategy is one that aligns well with the environment.

Notes:

_____

_____

_____

_____

B. **The primary steps in the strategic management process**

1. **Step 3**

After analyzing the environment, management can evaluate what opportunities it can exploit and threats that it faces.

Notes:

_____

_____

_____

_____

2. **Step 4**

Analyzing the organization's resources involves looking at the organization's skills and resources.

Notes:

_____

_____

_____

_____

3. **Step 5**

The analysis in step 4 should lead to a clear evaluation of the firm's strengths and weaknesses. Management can then identify the organization's *distinctive competence* or the unique skills and resources that determine the organization's competitive weapons.

Notes:

_____

_____

_____

_____

C. **Reassessing the organization's mission and objectives**

Step 6

A *SWOT analysis* is an analysis of an organization's strengths/weaknesses and its opportunities/threats. In light of the SWOT analysis, management may need to reassess the organization's mission and objectives.

Notes:

_____

_____

_____

_____

D. **Formulating strategies**

Step 7

Strategies need to be established at the corporate, business, and functional levels of the organization. In formulating strategies, management hopes to give the organization a competitive advantage. According to Michael Porter, managers choose from among three strategies—cost leadership, differentiation, and focus—according to the organization's strengths and the competitors' weaknesses.

Notes:

_____

_____

_____

_____

E. **Implementing the strategic management process**

1. **Step 8**

   Strategies must now be put into action. Strategic planning is only as good as the strategies that are properly implemented.

   Notes:

   _____

   _____

   _____

   _____

2. **Step 9**

   Managers must also evaluate results in order to know how effective their strategies have been and what corrections need to be made.

   Notes:

   _____

   _____

   _____

   _____

X.   **STRATEGY IS PART OF EVERY MANAGER'S JOB** — p. 72

Strategies help to give direction to the work that employees do. It is important that managers recognize that the general goals they set are distilled into more clearly defined work to be done by lower level managers. In the end, the strategy assists managers in day-to-day decision making.

Notes:

_____

_____

_____

_____

XI.   **TQM AS A STRATEGIC WEAPON?** — p. 73

A number of organization are using TQM as a way to build a sustainable competitive advantage.

Notes:

_____

_____

_____

_____

XII.   **ENTREPRENEURSHIP: A SPECIAL CASE OF STRATEGIC PLANNING** — p. 74

Many of the strategic planning concepts can be applied directly to those who are interested in entrepreneurship.

A. **What is entrepreneurship?**

There are numerous definitions to the term. In the text, *entrepreneurship* is defined as a process by which individuals pursue opportunities, fulfilling needs and wants through innovation, without regard to the resources they currently control.

Notes:

_____

_____

_____

_____

B. **Similar characteristics**

A number of characteristics of entrepreneurs have been identified in research studies.

1. High need for achievement.

2. Strong belief that they control their own destinies.

3. Moderate risk takers.

4. Independent types who prefer to be personally responsible.

5.   Two conclusions are evident:

   a.   People with this personality makeup are not likely to be contented, productive employees in the typical large organization or government agency.

   b.   The challenges and conditions inherent in starting one's own business mesh well with the entrepreneurial personality.

Notes:

_____

_____

_____

_____

C.   Entrepreneurs vs. traditional managers

There are some key differences between entrepreneurs and traditional bureaucratic managers.

Notes:

_____

_____

_____

_____

✓ ANSWERS TO REVIEW AND DISCUSSION QUESTIONS

1. *Contrast formal with informal planning.*

    The planning discussed in this chapter is of a formal nature. That is, it is written down and objectives are shared with others in the organization. All managers engage in planning, but it may only be of an informal nature. These plans aren't written down or shared with others.

2. *How does planning affect an organization in terms of performance? In terms of eliminating change? Are these effects altered if the planning proves to be inaccurate?*

    Planning has been shown through various research to be related to higher performance, but not in all cases. Generally speaking, formal planning is associated with higher profits, return on assets, and other positive financial results. When planning does not lead to higher performance, it is typically because the environment constrains options.

    Planning can't eliminate change. Changes are going to happen whether planning is taking place or not. However, planning can consider the possibilities of change and provide alternative scenarios for the various situations.

    Even if planning proves to be inaccurate, it still can be valuable. Planning provides direction and purpose. It minimizes misdirected energy. Thus, even though the result may miss the target, the clarification that planning provides is valuable to organizations and managers.

3. *Describe the six different types of plans discussed in this chapter.*

    Under the category of breadth, we have strategic and operational plans. Strategic plans refer to plans that are organization-wide, establish overall objectives, and position an organization in terms of its environment. An operational plan is a plan that specifies details on how overall objectives are to be achieved.

    Under the category of time frame, we have short-term and long-term plans. Short-term plans are plans that cover less than one year. Long-term plans are those that extend beyond five years.

    Under the category of specificity, we have specific and directional plans. Specific plans are plans that are clearly defined and leave no room for interpretation. Directional plans are flexible plans that set out general guidelines.

4. *How does the planning done by a top executive differ from that performed by a supervisor?*

For the most part, operational planning will dominate the planning activities of lower-level managers/supervisors. As managers go up through the levels of the organization, their planning role becomes more strategy-oriented.

5. *How does environmental uncertainty affect planning?*

The greater the environmental uncertainty, the more plans should be directional with emphasis placed on the short-term. When rapid or critical environmental changes are taking place, well-defined and precisely charted plans are more likely to hinder an organization's performance.

6. *Compare an organization's mission with its objectives.*

A mission defines the organization purpose. It is broad and answers the question: What business or businesses are we in. Objectives are more detailed. They translate the mission into concrete terms.

7. *Describe the nine-step strategic management process.*

In the nine-step strategic management process, managers identify the organization's current mission, objectives, and strategies; analyze the environment; identify threats and opportunities; analyze the organization's resources; identify the organization's strengths and weaknesses; reassess the organization's mission and objectives; formulate strategies; implement strategies; and evaluate results.

8. *What is a SWOT analysis?*

A SWOT analysis, the sixth step in the strategic management process, is an analysis of an organization's strengths, weaknesses, opportunities, and threats. Managers may consider reassessing the organization's mission and objectives in light of the results of a SWOT analysis.

9. *How would you describe Wal-Mart's competitive advantage in its industry?*

Wal-mart's competitive advantage would stem from its image which entails such aspects as low price with high quality and customer service.

10. ***All managers are involved in the strategic planning process. Describe how this happens.***

All managers become involved in different stages of the strategic planning process. Top managers set broad goals, middle managers translate the goals into specific work, and lower level managers make sure the work gets done.

11. ***How can TQM provide a competitive advantage?***

Recall that TQM focuses on quality and continuous improvement. To the degree that an organization can satisfy a customer's need for quality, it can differentiate itself from the competition and attract and hold a loyal customer base. Also, constant improvement in the quality and reliability of an organization's products or services can result in a competitive advantage that others can't imitate easily.

12. ***Are all small business managers entrepreneurs? Explain your answer.***

No, not all small business managers are entrepreneurs. Many do not innovate. Also, many managers of small businesses are merely scaled-down versions of the conservative, conforming bureaucrats who staff numerous large corporations and public agencies.

✓ SUGGESTIONS FOR DISCUSSING BOXED MATERIAL

Linda Hamilton of Hamilton & Scarpati Accounting Firm: What factors were inherent in the role Linda Hamilton played? Was she just lucky, or did she have identifiable managerial skills?

Peter Drucker's Management by Objectives: So, does MBO work? Ask students how they would feel as employees in an MBO environment and as managers. Would they want to manage by objective?

Is "Going Bankrupt" an Unethical Strategy?: Under what conditions would going bankrupt be ethical, and under what conditions would it be unethical? Who does such a strategy help? Who does it hurt? What are the long-term consequences? Be sure and point out that the discussion is particular to the United States, because many other countries do not allow for such options.

Michael Porter's Generic Strategies: Perhaps begin a discussion of how students respond as customers to organizations with cost advantages. What have they witnessed in the marketplace. Wal-Mart is a good example, considering that many communities are resisting it in light of its impact on other businesses. Is cost-leadership a good strategy? What are its weaknesses? When might it not work?

Steps in Goal Setting: Ask students how they feel about these steps? Do they agree? Do they translate on a personal level? In other words, how could these steps be revised in order to advise managers on setting their personal goals?

✓ SUGGESTIONS FOR THE SELF-ASSESSMENT EXERCISE

This self assessment attempts to identify how well your students plan. After completing the assessment and scoring it, groups can be established to answer the following questions:

* How do these statements affect your planning efforts?

* If you are a good planner, how did you learn to do it?

* If you are not yet a good planner, how can you make yourself a better planner?

* Did you get any insights/career implications from this assessment? What did you discover about yourself?

✓ COMMENTS ON CLASS EXERCISE

This case can lead to a very thought-provoking discussion.

* Consider assigning groups and having students meet before class and come prepared to give their presentations to the whole class.

* Suggest that students begin by thinking about schools in general.

* Then suggest that students refer to promotional materials that the school puts out, such as admissions materials.

* You may want to hand out copies of the Porter model that students can fill in with regard to their school.

✓ ANSWERS TO CASE APPLICATION QUESTIONS

1. ***Develop a strategy to help Topps cope with the changing environment it faces.***

    A good strategy will recognize the changing economy and account for other such changes in the future. Topps will have to decide if it should attempt to recapture its past audience or if it should target a new audience. Part of this analysis should take into account what the competitors are doing and are likely to do. In addition, the strategy should address the degree of Topps' diversification. A possible strategy could be to do nothing, as long as there is some defense of why Topps should not actively respond to the changing environment (this would probably be a weak answer).

2. ***Michael Porter identified three generic strategies that companies follow. What one of the three do you believe Topps should use? Discuss and support your choice.***

    Focus would appear to be the appropriate strategy for Topps in that, according to the case, demand in general has dropped. There is not much information on competitors, but it appears that they are not the problem for Topps, particularly since neither cost nor brand recognition appears to have been important in motivating buyers.

✓ SUGGESTIONS FOR USING VIDEO CASE

"Airlines and Planning in a Dynamic Environment"

Running Time: 8:00

This video case provides a good look at the airline industry that, for the past 15 years, has been buffeted by rapid and distinct environmental forces. None of the airlines has been immune from the chaos that characterizes this industry.

Use this video case as either an introduction or as a conclusion to the chapter. As an introduction, emphasize the chaotic nature of the industry and how airline managers have attempted to adapt to the changes. As a conclusion to your discussion of the chapter material, have students consider where and how planning could have been employed.

ANSWERS TO QUESTIONS

1. ***Is it possible for airline managers to engage in long-term planning in this environment? Discuss.***

    It would be very difficult for airline managers to engage in long-term planning in this type of environment. Long-term planning (plans that extend beyond five years) is least effective in highly dynamic and uncertain environments. In order to plan effectively, this type of time frame requires some assumptions that the environment will not be changing rapidly. This was not the situation here.

2. ***What kind of plans would be most effective for an airline operating in 1974? 1994? Explain.***

    In 1974, deregulation had not yet occurred, so airline managers could develop long-term and specific plans. The environment was predictable and relatively stable. However, in 1994, plans need to be short-term and directional in nature. As environmental factors change, the airlines' plans can be altered to meet the demands of the changed environment.

3. ***How might a contingency approach to planning be used for managers in the airline industry?***

A contingency approach to planning would be a necessity for managers in the airline industry. These managers would need to be cognizant of environmental changes and be prepared with alternative plans for different types of scenarios.

CHAPTER 4   PLANNING TOOLS AND TECHNIQUES

✓ LECTURE OUTLINE

✓ ANNOTATED OUTLINE

I.   **INTRODUCTION** — p. 81

This chapter introduces a number of the basic planning tools and techniques that can assist managers in their activities. In addition, a very practical and personal planning tool, time management, is presented at the end of the chapter.

Notes:

_____

_____

_____

_____

II. **ASSESSING THE ENVIRONMENT** — p. 81

A.   **Environmental scanning** involves the screening of much information to detect emerging trends and create scenarios. It is used by both large and small organizations. Two specific techniques are described next.

Notes:

_____

_____

_____

_____

B.   **Competitor intelligence** is an environmental scanning activity that seeks to identify who competitors are, what they're doing, and how their actions will affect the focus organization.

Notes:

_____

_____

_____

_____

C.   A **scenario** is a consistent view of what the future is likely to be. Developing scenarios allows management to see the impact of different assumptions on outcomes.

Notes:

_____

_____

_____

_____

D. **Forecasting** involves developing forecasts which are predictions of future outcomes.

   1. There are two popular *types of forecasts*.

      a. *Revenue forecasting* is predicting future revenues.

      b. *Technological forecasting* is predicting changes in technology and when new technologies are likely to be economically feasible.

   Notes:

_____

_____

_____

_____

   2. There are also two categories of *forecasting techniques*.

      a. *Quantitative forecasting* applies a set of mathematical rules to a series of past data to predict future outcomes.

      b. *Qualitative forecasting* involves judgment and opinions of knowledgeable individuals to predict future outcomes.

   Notes:

_____

_____

_____

_____

   3. *Forecasting effectiveness* is affected by the following elements.

      a. Forecasting techniques are most accurate in a static environment.

      b. Some suggestions for improving forecasting effectiveness are as follows:

         1. Use simple forecasting techniques.

2. Compare every forecast with "no change."

3. Don't rely on a single forecasting method.

4. Don't assume that you can accurately identify turning points in a trend.

5. Shorten the length of the forecasts.

Notes:

_____

_____

_____

_____

E. **Benchmarking** is defined as the search for the best practice among competitors or noncompetitors that lead to their superior performance. The benchmarking process typically follows four steps.

1. The organization forms a benchmarking team whose initial task is to identify what is to be benchmarked, identify comparative organizations, and determine data collection methods.

2. The team collects internal and external data.

3. The data is analyzed to identify performance gaps and to determine the cause of the difference.

4. An action plan is prepared and implemented.

Notes:

_____

_____

_____

_____

III. **BUDGETS** — p. 87

A *budget* is a numerical plan for allocating resources to specific activities. Budgets are popular because they are applicable to a wide variety of organizations and units within an organization.

A. **Types of budgets**. There are six different types of budgets.

1. A *revenue budget* is a budget that projects future sales.

2. An *expense budget* is a budget that lists the primary activities undertaken by a unit and allocates a dollar amount to each.

3. A *profit budget* is a budget used by separate units of an organization that combines revenue and expense budgets to determine the unit's profit contribution.

4. A *cash budget* is a budget that forecasts how much cash an organization will have on hand and how much it will need to meet expenses.

5. A *capital expenditures budget* is a budget that forecasts investments in property, buildings, and major equipment.

6. Most of the previous budgets are fixed; that is, they assume a fixed level of sales or production. The final type of budget is a *variable budget* which is a budget that takes into account those costs that vary with volume.

Notes:

_____

_____

_____

_____

B. **Approaches to budgeting.** There are basically two approaches that managers can take to budgeting.

1. An *incremental budget* is a budget that allocates funds to departments according to allocations in the previous period.

2. *Zero-based budgeting (ZBB)* is a system in which budget requests start from scratch, regardless of previous appropriations.

Notes:

_____

_____

_____

_____

IV. **OPERATIONAL PLANNING TOOLS** — p. 90

A. **Scheduling** involves a listing of necessary activities, their order of accomplishment, who is to do each, and time needed to complete them. Some useful scheduling devices include the following.

1. *The Gantt chart*, named after Henry Gantt, visually shows when tasks are supposed to be done and compares that to the actual progress on each.

2. A *load chart* is a modified Gantt chart that schedules capacity by work stations.

3. *PERT network analysis* is useful for complicated projects. PERT (Program Evaluation and Review Technique) is a technique for scheduling complex projects comprising many activities, some of which are interdependent. A PERT network is a flowchart-like diagram that depicts the sequence of activities needed to complete a project and the time or costs associated with each activity.

    a. *Events* are end points that represent the completion of major activities in a PERT network.

    b. *Activities* are the time or resources needed to progress from one event to another in a PERT network.

    c. The *critical path* is the longest sequence of activities in a PERT network.

Notes:

_____

_____

_____

_____

B. **Break-even analysis** is a technique for identifying the point at which total revenue is just sufficient to cover total costs.

Notes:

_____

_____

_____

_____

C. **Linear programming** is a mathematical technique that can be used to solve resource allocation problems.

Notes:

_____

_____

_____

_____

D. **Queuing theory** is a technique that balances the cost of having a waiting line against the cost of service to maintain that line.

Notes:

_____

_____

_____

_____

✓ ANSWERS TO REVIEW AND DISCUSSION QUESTIONS

1. *How is scanning the environment related to forecasting?*

   Scanning the environment helps an organization to anticipate changes that may occur in the environment. Once these have been identified, management can project into the future various scenarios, based on their past experiences.

2. *Assume that you manage a large fast food restaurant in downtown Philadelphia, and you want to know the amount of each type of sandwich to make and the number of cashiers to have on each shift. What type of planning tool(s) do you think will be useful to you? What type of environmental scanning will you need to do to implement the tool(s) you use?*

   Planning tools that would be most appropriate include probability theory and queuing theory. Probability theory can be used to analyze past predictable patterns in the ordering of different types of sandwiches. Queuing theory could be used to help determine the number of cashiers to have on each shift by balancing the cost of having a waiting line against the cost of opening another line with another cashier.

   Appropriate techniques for scanning the environment would include reading newspapers, magazines, books, and trade journals; reading competitors' ads, promotional materials and press releases; attending trade shows; and reverse engineering of competitors' products.

3. *What is a scenario and how does competitor intelligence help managers to formulate one?*

   A scenario is a consistent view of what the future is likely to be. Competitor intelligence could help managers formulate scenarios because it could identify who competitors are, what they're doing, and how their actions likely will affect the organization. Different scenarios could be developed for different assumptions about competitor actions.

4. *How can benchmarking improve the quality of an organization's products or processes?*

   The basic idea behind benchmarking is that management can improve quality of its products or processes by analyzing and then copying the methods of the leaders in various fields.

5. *What is a budget? Must it always be based on monetary units?*

A budget is a numerical plan that is both a planning and a controlling tool. Budgets need not always be based on monetary units since other elements such as time, space, or material resources can be budgeted.

6. *"Budgets are both a planning and control tool." Explain this statement.*

Budgets direct behavior by defining priorities. They set standards. These priorities and standards are criteria against which actual performance is measured and compared (control).

7. *Develop a Gantt chart for writing a college term paper.*

Student responses to this will vary somewhat. However, the Gantt chart should identify the key activities (topic selection, research in library, rough draft, etc.), the time necessary for completion of each activity, the order in which the tasks need to be completed, and then the charting of this information.

8. *What is the significance of the critical path in a PERT network?*

The critical path identifies the longest or most time-consuming sequence of events and activities in a PERT network. Thus, if an activity on the critical path is delayed, all other things being equal, so too will the project be delayed. Accordingly, the critical path helps to identify significant control points for management.

9. *What is the value of break-even analysis as a planning tool?*

Break-even analysis reveals the relationship among revenues, costs, and profits. It instructs a manager on how many units of production the organization needs to sell to cover fixed costs. It can also help in determining if a current product line should be continued or dropped from the organization's product line.

10. *How can queuing theory serve to make an operation more efficient?*

Queuing theory can make an operation more efficient by determining the level of servers needed. Queuing theory balances the costs of having a waiting line against the costs incurred in maintaining that line to help managers plan for the level of service they want to provide.

✔ SUGGESTIONS FOR DISCUSSING BOXED MATERIAL

Larry Harmon of Demar Plumbing: What were the keys to Larry Harmon's success? Should customer satisfaction always come first? Ask students to point to situations during recent years where they have noticed companies putting the customer first. For example, Wal-Mart offers to refund the difference to any customer who can find a product at a lower price at another store.

When Does Competitive Intelligence Become Espionage?: Ask students to discuss what sorts of policies they would put into place to guide employees' information-gathering efforts?

Texas Instrument's Zero-Based Budgeting Technique: This material provides you an opportunity to go over the budgeting technique in more detail. You can make sure students understand it by discussing its advantages and disadvantages.

Five Steps to Better Time Management: Ask students if they agree with these steps. What other steps do they find helpful? As managers, how could they help their employees manage their time better? What advice would they offer?

✔ SUGGESTIONS FOR THE SELF-ASSESSMENT EXERCISE

This self assessment exercise focuses on one's tendency to be an entrepreneur. After scoring, assign students who have similar scores into groups. In these groups, students should discuss the following questions:

* Do you agree with your assessment scoring? Why or why not?

* How would you explain the results of your assessment scoring?

* How could this information be useful? How could this information not be useful?

* What are the career implications of such an assessment?

✓ COMMENTS ON CLASS EXERCISE

The purpose of this exercise is to get students to see planning as a similar activity, regardless of the specific objectives. Consider posing the following questions to students after they complete the exercise:

* What similarities did you find in how you planned for different objectives?

* Could PERT be used to help you manage your time better?

* Can you think of other ways you might be able to use PERT?

✓ ANSWERS TO CASE APPLICATION QUESTIONS

1. *Draw a PERT network of this program.*

   A   B   E

                    G

   C   D   F

2. *Calculate the expected time for each activity and include it in the PERT network.*

   $t_e A =$ 6 weeks

   $t_e B =$ 22 weeks

   $t_e C =$ 4 weeks

   $t_e D =$ 7 weeks

   $t_e E =$ 5 weeks

   $t_e F =$ 2 weeks

   $t_e G =$ 6 weeks

3. *How long should this program take?*

   The following paths could be followed:

A - B - F - G = 36

A - B - E - G = 39

C - D - F - G = 19

C - D - E - G = 22

This program should take about 39 weeks according to **expected** time. It would be about 25.5 weeks according to optimistic time. It should **take** about 37.50 weeks according to most likely time. Finally, it should take about 58.5 weeks according to pessimistic time.

4. *What's the critical path in this program? What are the implications of delays in activities along this path?*

The critical path falls on the path with activities A - B - E - G for a total of 39 weeks (expected time). If any of these critical activities (A or B or E or G) are delayed, it will take longer than 39 weeks to complete the project.

✓ SUGGESTIONS FOR USING VIDEO CASE

"Smart Highways and Cars Help Commuters Plan Their Journeys"

Running Time: 5:03

This video case provides an interesting look into the role of technology. In this instance, technology promises to translate queuing theory into time, fuel, and road safety savings. It's as if the state/government is the business, the roads are the servers, and drivers are the customers.

The video case works well as an introduction to the chapter, in that it shows students how careful planning can provide concrete results. It also works well as a conclusion. The chapter is full of theories and calculations. This case shows that they can work. In addition, you may want to consider returning to this case when you get to chapters 15 and 16. At that point you may want to question the role of technology in society and speculate about what's next.

ANSWERS TO QUESTIONS

1. *How is queuing theory evident in the functioning of smart highways?*

    Queuing theory involves balancing the costs of having a waiting line against the costs of adding services. In the case of highways, the costs involve the wear-and-tear on the roads as well as the costs to individuals having to wait. Also involved are the social fuel and pollution costs. Added to this is the waste if roads that could be used aren't being used.

    Queuing theory assumes that servers (in this case, roads) all serve at their capacity. The functioning of smart highways helps to spread out the business (traffic) as evenly as possible across all possible servers (roads).

2. *In what ways will smart highways and cars assist individuals in their driving plans?*

    Smart highways and cars will tell drivers which "servers" are free (which roads are not as busy as others). It will help them save time and money on gas.

3. *What potential problems do you think smart highways and cars may face in the next decade? How might they be addressed?*

Resistance to dependence on technology and vulnerability to power outages are always potential problems. This problems will be addressed inherently as people save time on the roads. At the same time, however, it will be important to minimize people's expectations. Technology can only do what is physically allowed. In other words, for people to feel the decrease in traffic, there will have to be enough roads that people are willing to use.

CHAPTER 5   FOUNDATIONS OF DECISION MAKING

✓ LECTURE OUTLINE

GROUP DECISION MAKING

EFFECT OF NATIONAL CULTURE ON DECISION-MAKING STYLES — p. 120

SUMMARY — p. 121

✓ ANNOTATED OUTLINE

I. **INTRODUCTION** — p. 104

All managers make numerous decisions. The overall quality of these decisions strongly affect the organization's success or failure. The concept of decision making is explored in this chapter.

Notes:

_____

_____

_____

_____

II. **PLANNING AND DECISION MAKING** — p. 104

Plans result from careful analyses. Managers go through an extensive process of identifying and evaluating various options from which they select those that best serve the interests of the organization. This selection process is called decision making.

Notes:

_____

_____

_____

_____

III. **THE DECISION MAKING PROCESS** — p. 105

Decision making is a process that involves more than the simple act of choosing among alternatives. The *decision-making process* is defined as a set of eight steps that include identifying a problem, selecting an alternative, and evaluating the decision's effectiveness.

A. A **problem** is defined as a discrepancy between an existing and a desired state of affairs. Some cautions about problem identification include the following:

1. Make sure it's a problem and not just a symptom of a problem.

2. Problem identification is subjective.

3. Before a problem can be determined, a manager must be aware of any discrepancies.

4. Discrepancies can be found by comparing current results with some standard.

5. Pressure must be exerted on the manager to correct the discrepancy.

6. Managers aren't likely to characterize some discrepancy as a problem if they perceive that they don't have the authority, money, information, or other resources needed to act on it.

Notes:

_____

_____

_____

_____

B. The **decision criteria** include any criteria that define what is relevant in a decision.

Notes:

_____

_____

_____

_____

C. The criteria identified must be **weighted** in order to give them correct priority in the decision.

Notes:

_____

_____

_____

_____

D. The decision maker now needs to **identify viable alternatives** for resolving the problem.

Notes:

_____

_____

_____

_____

E. Each of the alternatives must now be critically **analyzed**. Each alternative is evaluated by appraising it against the criteria.

Notes:

_____

_____

_____

_____

F. The act of selecting the **best alternative** from among those identified and assessed is critical.

Notes:

_____

_____

_____

_____

G. The chosen alternative must be **implemented**. Implementation is defined as conveying a decision to those affected and getting their commitment to it.

Notes:

_____

_____

_____

_____

H. The last step in the decision-making process **evaluates the effectiveness** of the result of the decision to see whether or not the problem has been corrected.

_____

_____

_____

_____

IV.   **RATIONAL DECISION MAKING** — p. 109

Rational decision making describes choices that are consistent and value-maximizing within specific constraints.

A. **Assumptions of rationality.** There are seven assumptions about rationality.

1. The problem is clear and unambiguous.

2. A single, well-defined goal is to be achieved.

3. All alternatives and consequences are known.

4. Preferences are clear.

5. Preferences are constant and stable.

6. No time or cost constraints exist.

7. Final choice will maximize economic payoff.

Notes:

_____

_____

_____

_____

B. **Limits to rationality.** Unfortunately, most decisions that managers face don't meet all the tests of rationality. Studies into the decision-making process have uncovered some important insights.

Notes:

_____

_____

_____

_____

C.	**Bounded rationality** is defined as behavior that is rational within the parameters of a simplified model that captures the essential features of a problem. The result of bounded rationality is *satisficing*, which is defined as acceptance of solutions that are "good enough."

Notes:

_____
_____
_____
_____

V.	**DECISION MAKING: A CONTINGENCY APPROACH** — p. 111

Since the type of problem a manager faces in a decision-making situation can influence how the problem is addressed, a categorization scheme for problems and types of decisions is presented next.

A.	**Types of problems**. Well-structured problems are straightforward, familiar, and easily defined problems. Ill-structured problems are new problems in which information is ambiguous or incomplete.

Notes:

_____
_____
_____
_____

B.	**Types of decisions**. There are two types of decisions that managers might face.

1.	*Programmed decisions* are repetitive decisions that can be handled by a routine approach. In dealing with this type of decision, managers may utilize procedures, rules, or policies.

a.	A procedure is a series of interrelated sequential steps that can be used to respond to a structured problem.

b.	A rule is an explicit statement that tells managers what they ought or ought not to do.

c.	A policy is a guide that establishes parameters for making decisions.

2.	*Nonprogrammed decisions* are unique decisions that require a custom-made solution.

Notes:

_____

_____

_____

_____

C. **Integration**. Lower-level managers typically confront familiar and repetitive problems and rely on programmed decisions. As managers move up the levels of the organization, the problems tend to become more ill-structured. However, few managerial decisions in the real world are either fully programmed or nonprogrammed.

Notes:

_____

_____

_____

_____

VI. **GROUP DECISION MAKING**

A. **Advantages and disadvantages**. Individual and group decisions each have their own set of strengths and drawbacks.

1. The *advantages* that group decisions have over individuals include the following:

   a. Provides more complete information.

   b. Generates more alternatives.

   c. Increases acceptance of a situation.

   d. Increases legitimacy.

2. The *drawbacks* include the following:

   a. Time consuming.

   b. Minority domination.

   c. Pressures to conform which can lead to groupthink.

   d. Ambiguous responsibility.

_____

_____

_____

_____

B. **Effectiveness and efficiency**. Are groups more effective than individuals? It depends on the criteria used for defining effectiveness.

1. Group decisions tend to be more accurate.

2. Individual decisions are quicker in terms of speed.

3. Group decisions tend to have more acceptance.

4. The effectiveness of group decisions tends to be influenced by the size of the group. Groups should not be too large.

5. Groups also are not as efficient as individual decision makers.

Notes:

_____

_____

_____

_____

C. **Techniques for improving group decision making**. There are four ways to make group decisions more creative.

1. *Brainstorming* is an idea-generating process that encourages alternatives while withholding criticism.

2. *Nominal group technique* is a decision-making technique in which group members are physically present but operate independently.

3. *Delphi technique* is a group decision-making technique in which members never meet face to face.

4. *Electronic meetings* are decision-making groups that interact by way of linked computers.

Notes:

_____

_____

_____

_____

VII. **EFFECT OF NATIONAL CULTURE ON DECISION-MAKING STYLES —**
p. 120

Managers need to modify their decision styles to reflect the organizational culture
where they work. In addition, since the decision variables, such as risk aversity and
preferred group size, vary by culture, managers should also modify their decision
styles to reflect the national culture of the country where they live.

Notes:

_____

_____

_____

_____

✓ ANSWERS TO REVIEW AND DISCUSSION QUESTIONS

1. *Explain how decision making is related to the planning process.*

   Careful decision making lies at the heart of well-crafted plans. Plans do not come out of the air. Decision making is implied in the planning process.

2. *Describe a decision you have made that closely aligns with the assumptions of perfect rationality. Compare this with the process you used to select your college. Is there a deviation? Why?*

   Answers to this question will vary widely. Focus and attention should be placed, however, on two areas: the eight step decision-making process and the deviations. Most students simplified the college decision by looking at only 3 or 4 alternatives and using a short list of criteria.

3. *What are the steps of the rational decision-making model?*

   There are eight steps in the rational decision-making model: (1) formulation of a problem, (2) identification of decision criteria, (3) allocation of weights to the criteria, (4) development of alternatives, (5) analysis of alternatives, (6) selection of an alternative, (7) implementation of the alternative, and (8) evaluation of decision effectiveness.

4. *How is implementation important to the decision-making process?*

   The decision must be put into action. This is where implementation comes in. Implementation is defined as conveying a decision to those affected and getting their commitment to it.

5. *What is a satisficing decision?*

   A satisficing decision is one that is "good enough." It meets the decision maker's criteria of being both satisfactory and sufficient. Rather than optimizing, it meets the minimum threshold test.

6. *Why might a manager use a simplified decision model?*

A simplified decision model might be used by managers as a means of responding to the complexity of their tasks by reducing problems to a level which is readily understood. This simplified model may also reflect decisions where perfect rationality does not exist; self-interests of the decision maker are considered; or the organization's culture, internal politics, or power considerations warrant its use.

7. *What's the difference between a rule and a policy?*

A rule is an explicit statement that tells a manager what he or she ought or ought not to do. A policy provides guidelines to channel a manager's thinking in a specific direction. Thus, the policy establishes parameters for the decision maker instead of specifically stating what should or should not be done.

8. *Is the order in which alternatives are considered more critical under assumptions of perfect rationality or bounded rationality? Why?*

The order of alternatives is more critical in the realistic model (bounded rationality) because, unlike the rational model where all alternatives are evaluated and the optimal one chosen, once a satisfactory alternative is identified under the bounded rationality model, it is accepted.

9. *What is groupthink? What are its implications for decision making?*

Groupthink represents conformity to outside pressures and the withholding of deviant, minority, or unpopular views, thus causing members to suffer deterioration of mental efficiency, reality testing, and moral judgments. Its major implication for decision making is that it can create poorly thought-out decisions.

10. *Why do you think organizations have increased the use of groups for making decisions during the past 20 years? When would you recommend using groups to make decisions?*

The primary emphasis appears to be an outgrowth of the human resources school of management. Employee participation in matters that affect them have been strongly advocated. Accordingly, in those organizations where increased input for ideas is needed, increased acceptance of decisions is necessary, and increased employee commitment to management practices is important, many organizations have gone to a group decision-making practice.

There are an abundant number of reasons for using group decisions—some good, some not so good. The obvious advantages of group decision making include accuracy, acceptance, and creativity. In essence, except where speed is critical or maintaining manager power is desired, a good case can be made that group decisions are more effective and thus should be used.

✓ SUGGESTIONS FOR DISCUSSING BOXED MATERIAL

Should Social Responsibility Play a Factor in the Decision to Relocate a Plant or Headquarters' Office?: You may want to have students discuss the variety of factors that inevitably come into play concerning the location or relocation of facilities. What factors should come into play, and which should be excluded?

Herbert Simon and Bounded Rationality: How do students feel about this? Does it make sense that managers gravitate toward highly visible solutions? You may want to ask students to think of real-world examples where this has apparently been the case. Are there examples to the contrary?

Yasuo Kikuta of Fujitsu Ltd.: It is important that students recognize the inevitable role of factors such as sex, race, and nationality. What role have such factors played in this manager's career? Does success mean that the factors don't matter?

Irving L. Janis and Groupthink: Have students talk about situations where groupthink was present. Ask students to cite real examples and offer suggestions as to how groupthink could have been minimized.

Conducting a Group Meeting: These are very broad guidelines. How do students react? Are they specific enough? Perhaps have students come up with a more specific list during the class discussion.

✓ SUGGESTIONS FOR THE SELF-ASSESSMENT EXERCISE

This self-assessment exercise is a measure of your intuitive ability. It is possible that intuition can facilitate the manager's decision-making process. Have students take the self-assessment and score it. Then students can either be paired off or work individually on the following questions:

* Are you surprised by your score? Why or why not?

* What impact/implications might this information have for your career plans?

* Are there any particular items on the assessment that you would like to explore further? Which ones and why?

✓ COMMENTS ON CLASS EXERCISE

The purpose of this exercise is to get students to get a feel for the differences between group and individual decision making. In class, after the groups have met, you may want to have students explore the implications.

* Did the group outperform the average individual? Why or why not?

* What made the group perform effectively?

* What detracted from the group's performance?

* Under what conditions would a group be preferable to an individual for a decision to be made?

* Under what conditions would an individual be preferable to a group for a decision to be made?

✓ ANSWERS TO CASE APPLICATION QUESTIONS

1. *Using the rational decision-making process, analyze Anthony Frederick's decision to go into the motel business.*

   (1) Frederick's problem lay in having a lot to pay in taxes. (2) Decision-making criteria included risk, price, and tax benefit, among others (such as, desire to expand business). (3) Frederick apparently weighted tax benefit highly and was not risk averse. (4) The case does not mention alternatives, but it is likely he considered other purchases that would have always resulted in a tax benefit. (5) It is likely that he also considered alternatives in terms of riskiness and profitability. (6) The alternative of buying hotels was selected. (7) The purchase was made. (8) The effectiveness became apparent with the downturn in the economy.

2. *How did poor decision making lead to Frederick's troubles?*

   The case does not specify, but it appears that Frederick may not have considered and evaluated alternatives adequately. This could have caused his loss, or it could have just been bad luck.

3. *Analyze the decision Frederick made in expanding Frederick Seal to a full-service company in terms of bounded rationality.*

   Frederick has accepted the limits of his rationality and knowledge. By expanding into the full-service arena, Frederick took what assets he had and decided to use them as best he could within the context of his failures.

✓ SUGGESTIONS FOR USING VIDEO CASE

"Explaining the Absence of Black College Football Coaches"

Running Time: 8:01

This video case covers an area that should prove particularly interesting to most college students. College athletic programs are often the source of much controversy both on a particular campus and across the nation. In this video, we find an interesting discussion about the absence of black college football coaches.

This case could be used either as an introduction to the chapter on decision making or at the end of discussion of the chapter. As an introduction, emphasize that decision making permeates every aspect of a manager's job and athletic directors are often put in the "hot seat" when making decisions about head coaching jobs. As a conclusion to the chapter, ask students to particularly note *how* decisions are made in these situations.

ANSWERS TO QUESTIONS

1. *Why has gender-equity become a problem for the NCAA but not the absence of black head coaches?*

   A problem is defined as a discrepancy between an existing and a desired state of affairs. The absence of black head coaches has not been perceived as a problem for the NCAA probably because there are already black head coaches at 10 percent of the NCAA's top 300 schools. Also, there are many black assistant coaches who critics claim only have to "wait their turn" and to "do their job" to be considered head coaches.

2. *What criteria do athletic directors appear to be using in their decisions and how does this affect their decision outcomes?*

   The video suggests that the decision makers—the athletic directors—are concerned that the head football coach is such a visible member of the university community and that many communities are "not ready" for this individual to be black. Also, the "old boys network" of referrals is sometimes given as a reason since these "old boys" tend to be white males who call their friends and acquaintances for recommendations. Therefore, the decision criteria that athletic directors appear to be using are: who will the community accept and who can I call for recommendations. These types of criteria will undoubtedly affect their decision outcomes by limiting the potential alternatives.

3. *Is this an example of groupthink? Are athletic directors, presidents, and others who participate in the decisions to hire coaches risk-aversive? Discuss.*

This situation potentially could be perceived as an example of groupthink. Groupthink is defined as the withholding by group members of different views in order to appear to be in agreement. It appears that none of the individuals involved in this highly-visible decision process wants to appear out of sync with the rest of the group. It is hard to say whether athletic directors, presidents, and others who participate in the hiring process are risk-aversive. The group may be willing to take a risk on an unknown individual—as long as he is a white male.

$\mathcal{P}$art 3

CHAPTER 6   FOUNDATIONS OF ORGANIZING

✓ LECTURE OUTLINE

✓ ANNOTATED OUTLINE

I.   **INTRODUCTION** — p. 127

The right organizational structure can play an important role in an organization's evolution. This chapter introduces the elements of organizational structure.

Notes:

_____

_____

_____

_____

II. **WHAT IS ORGANIZATION STRUCTURE?** — p. 128

There are several definitions that must be understood as a precursor to understanding organizational structure and design.

Notes:

_____

_____

_____

_____

A. **Organization structure** is an organization's framework as expressed by its degree of complexity, formalization, and centralization.

Notes:

_____

_____

_____

_____

B. **Complexity** is defined as the amount of differentiation in an organization.

_____

_____

_____

_____

C.   **Formalization** is the degree to which an organization relies on rules and
      procedures to direct the behavior of employees.

      Notes:

      _____

      _____

      _____

      _____

D.   **Centralization** is defined as the concentration of decision-making authority in
      upper management.

      Notes:

      _____

      _____

      _____

      _____

E.   **Decentralization** is the handing down of decision-making authority to lower
      levels in an organization.

      Notes:

      _____

      _____

      _____

      _____

F.   **Organization design** is the construction or changing of an organization's
      structure.

Notes:

_____

_____

_____

_____

III.   **BASIC ORGANIZATION DESIGN CONCEPTS** — p. 128

The classical concepts of organization design were devised by the general administrative theorists. Henri Fayol and others from this school of thought proposed a set of five basic classical principles for managers to follow in designing organizations.

Notes:

_____

_____

_____

_____

A. **Division of labor** describes splitting a job into a number of steps with each step being completed by a separate individual.

1. In the *classical view* of division of labor, the diversity of skills that workers held were efficiently used. Also, division of labor was viewed as an unending source of increased productivity.

2. In the *contemporary view*, researchers began to recognize that there was a point at which the human diseconomies from division of labor exceeded the economic advantages. These human diseconomies took the form of boredom, fatigue, stress, low productivity, poor quality, increased absenteeism, and high turnover.

Notes:

_____

_____

_____

_____

B. **Unity of command** is defined as the principle that a subordinate should have one and only one superior to whom he or she is directly responsible.

1. In the *classical view*, unity of command was strictly adhered to. In the rare instance when the principle had to be violated, it was clearly designated that there be an explicit separation of activities and a supervisor responsible for each.

2. In the *contemporary view*, the unity of command principle is viewed as logical when organizations are simple. However, if situations warrant, the advantages of flexibility in structure that come from violating the unity of command principle far outweigh the disadvantages.

Notes:

_____

_____

_____

_____

C. **Authority and responsibility.** *Authority* is defined as the rights inherent in a managerial position to give orders and expect them to be obeyed. *Responsibility* is defined as an obligation to perform assigned activities.

1. In the *classical view*, authority was a major doctrine. It was viewed as the glue that held organizations together. Authority related to one's position within the organization. When authority was delegated, commensurate responsibility had to be allocated.

    a. Authority and responsibility needed to be equal.

    b. Responsibility cannot be delegated.

    c. The contradiction here was answered by recognizing two forms of responsibility: operating responsibility and ultimate responsibility.

    d. There were also two forms of authority relationships: *line authority* is the authority that entitles a manager to direct the work of a subordinate—it follows the *chain of command* which is the flow of authority from the top to the bottom of an organization; and *staff authority* which is authority that supports, assists, and advises holders of the authority.

2. In the *contemporary view*, we recognize that authority is only one element in the larger concept of power.

   a. *Power* is defined as the capacity to influence decisions.

   b. Power is diagrammed as a three-dimensional concept that includes functional, hierarchical, and centrality dimensions.

   c. Five sources of power have been identified by French and Raven:

      1. *Coercive power* is power that is dependent on fear.

      2. *Reward power* is power based on the ability to distribute anything that others may value.

      3. *Legitimate power* is power based on one's position in the formal hierarchy.

      4. *Expert power* is power based on one's expertise, special skill, or knowledge.

      5. *Referent power* is power based on identification with a person who has desirable resources or personal traits.

   Notes:

   _____

   _____

   _____

   _____

D. **Span of control** is defined as the number of subordinates a manager can direct efficiently and effectively.

   1. The *classical view* favored small spans, typically no more than six, in order to maintain close control.

   2. The *contemporary view* establishes that more and more organizations are increasing their spans of control. The span of control is increasingly being determined by looking at various contingency factors.

Notes:

_____

_____

_____

_____

E. **Departmentalization** is another area in which classical and contemporary views differ.

1. In the *classical view*, activities in the organization had to be specialized and grouped into departments. The approach to grouping selected should be the one that best contributes to the attainment of the organization's objectives and goals. There were five approaches to departmentalizing.

    a. *Functional departmentalization* grouped activities by functions performed.

    b. *Product departmentalization* grouped activities by product line.

    c. *Customer departmentalization* grouped activities on the basis of common customers.

    d. *Geographic departmentalization* grouped activities on the basis of territory.

    e. *Process departmentalization* grouped activities on the basis of product or customer flow.

Notes:

_____

_____

_____

_____

2. In the *contemporary view*, most large organizations continue to use most or all of the classical departmental groupings. However, two trends can be noted.

    a. Customer departmentalization is becoming increasingly emphasized.

    b. Rigid departmentalization is being complemented by the use of teams that cross over departmental lines.

Notes:

_____

_____

_____

_____

IV. **CONTINGENCY APPROACH TO ORGANIZATION DESIGN** — p. 140

Classical views of organization design were that the ideal structural design was a mechanistic/bureaucratic organization. We now recognize that the ideal organization design depends on contingency factors.

A. **Mechanistic and organic organizations**. Two diverse organizational forms can be described.

1. A *mechanistic organization* or *bureaucracy* is a structure that is high in complexity, formalization, and centralization.

2. An *organic organization* or *adhocracy* is a structure that is low in complexity, formalization, and centralization.

Notes:

_____

_____

_____

_____

B. **Strategy and structure**. Strategy and structure are closely linked, and as strategy changes, the structure should also.

Notes:

_____

_____

_____

_____

C. **Size and structure**. There is considerable historical evidence that an organization's size significantly affects its structure.

Notes:

_____

_____

_____

_____

D. **Technology and structure**. Every organization uses some form of technology to transform inputs into outputs. Two research studies on the relationship between technology and structure have been significant.

Notes:

_____

_____

_____

_____

E. **Environment and structure**. Research has shown that environment is a major influence on structure. We also know that mechanistic organizations tend to be ill-equipped to respond to rapid environmental change.

Notes:

_____

_____

_____

_____

V. ORGANIZATION STRUCTURE AND CULTURAL VALUES — p. 145

Organization structures should reflect the cultural values of the countries where they are located. It is important for managers to recognize that different cultures support different types of organizational structures.

Notes:

_____

_____

_____

_____

✓ ANSWERS TO REVIEW AND DISCUSSION QUESTIONS

1. *Can you reconcile the following two statements: (a) An organization should have as few levels as possible to foster coordination; and (b) An organization should have narrow spans of control to facilitate control.*

    These two statements reflect a basic contradiction in classical organization theory. Early writers advocated having as few levels in the hierarchy as possible and narrow spans of administration. These two views, when taken in the extreme, are incompatible.

2. *Which is more efficient—a wide or a narrow span of control? Why?*

    All other things being equal, a wide span is more efficient. This is true because it requires fewer managers. However, it is important to recognize that, at some point, effectiveness will decline.

3. *Why did the classical writers argue that authority should equal responsibility?*

    The classical writers argued that authority should equal responsibility so that managers were not responsible for outcomes over which they had no authority and to protect against excessive use of authority.

4. *Can the manager of a staff department have line authority? Explain.*

    Yes. Managers of staff departments have line authority over those individuals in their department who report directly to them.

5. *How are authority and organization structure related?*

    Authority provides the formal mechanism for decision making in organizations. It is explicitly encompassed in the centralization component of structure. If authority is concentrated at the top of an organization, then the organization is centralized. If authority is delegated down through the levels of the organization, then the organization is decentralized.

6. *What are the five sources of power?*

According to French and Raven, the five sources of power include reward (comes from ability to distribute anything that others may value), coercive (comes from fear), legitimate (comes from position in the formal hierarchy), expert (comes from expertise, special skill, or knowledge), and referent (comes from desirable resources or personal traits).

7. *Why is an understanding of power important?*

Understanding power is important because authority is a component of the larger concept of power. Power is defined as one's ability to influence decisions. That power can come from sources other than one's authority (or position) within the organization.

8. *In what ways can management departmentalize?*

Management can departmentalize by function, product or service, customer or client, geography, or process.

9. *Is your college organized as a mechanistic or an organic organization? Is this the type of structure you would ideally choose for it? Explain.*

The answer to this question depends on the college's strategy, size, technology, and environment. Is your college a liberal arts college or a multi-product university? Is your college large or small? Its technology probably would be nonroutine, and its environment dynamic. A college, at least in theory, should probably be designed around the organic form to reflect the dynamic nature of knowledge and the need to change courses to reflect this dynamic condition.

10. *Under what conditions is the mechanistic organization most effective? When is the organic organization most effective?*

A mechanistic organization is most effective when organizations have product diversification, large size, routine technologies, and stable environments. An organic organization is most effective when organizations have single-product strategies, small size, nonroutine technology, and high environmental uncertainty.

✓ SUGGESTIONS FOR DISCUSSING BOXED MATERIAL

Max Weber and the Ideal Structure: Bureaucracy?: Do you believe, as Weber believes, that organizations will be more rational and efficient if structured around structure/function, rewards, and individual rights. Ask students if they agree that career advancement would be based on individual qualifications. Are there examples of organizations that appear based on Weber's three characteristics?

Stanley Milgram and Following Orders: It is often useful to show the film that relates to the Milgram experiments because it helps to get students to buy in. It is often difficult to get the full effect when you just read about the experiments. On a more controversial note, depending upon the audience, it is also sometimes interesting to turn the discussion toward Hitler and compare what Milgram discovered to what Hitler's experience reveals.

Should You Follow Orders With Which You Don't Agree?: It is often difficult to distinguish between orders that are intrinsically wrong and orders you just happen to disagree with. Should employees always follow the orders of their managers? Under what circumstances would an employee be justified in not following his or her manager's orders? As a manager, how can you make sure employees follow your orders?

Building a Power Base: Is it always a good idea to build a power base. Can't some of these principles work against you? For example, it is possible to alienate co-workers by making yourself appear too indispensable.

Monte Peterson at Thermos: Do you agree that Peterson couldn't have caused such financial success within a bureaucracy? What is it about bureaucracy that could be construed as constraining? Are there ways to get around such elements without moving away from bureaucracy entirely? In what situations are bureaucracies viable alternatives?

✓ SUGGESTIONS FOR THE SELF-ASSESSMENT EXERCISE

This self-assessment exercise focuses on one's propensity (aptitude) for managing. Have students take the assessment and score it. Students could be divided into groups or work individually on the following questions:

* Why do you think you feel the way you do? Explain.

* How can you use this information in helping you to plan your career?

* Are there any similarities between this assessment and the results of your self-assessment exercise in Chapter 1? Explain.

✓ COMMENTS ON CLASS EXERCISE

The purpose of this exercise is to get students to think of organizations in terms of groups they are familiar with—their schools.

* What kind of structure did you predict your school had?

* What kind of structure do you now think it has?

* Is it an appropriate structure?

* If it were your decision, what type of structure would you have in place?

✓ ANSWERS TO CASE APPLICATION QUESTIONS

1. *How does a changing environment affect strategy? How did it at CMP?*

Managers must remain cognizant of environmental factors and be prepared to adjust strategy in order to compensate for changes in the environment. At CMP, managers had to deal with growth. While usually positive, growth presents numerous challenges that managers cannot ignore. CMP found that a larger organization was needed to handle the larger amount of business. With this in mind, a new structure was necessary as well.

2. *What benefits might Gerry and Lilo Leeds gain in reorganizing to a divisional structure?*

The divisional structure has enabled better communication within the company. In addition, it has facilitated decision making by decentralizing it and allowing lower level managers to make decisions. The primary benefit is that CMP is a thriving company that is capable of handling present and continued growth.

3. *In your opinion, how frequently should organizational members evaluate the company's structure in deciding if it should be altered?*

There is no set time limit. However, organizational members should evaluate their structures whenever there are significant changes in the environment or whenever there are significant turns in the organizational business.

✓ SUGGESTIONS FOR USING VIDEO CASE

"Cornrows and Company"

Running Time: 10:53

This video case is an example of a creative type of small business. It is also an example of how formal rules can work against creative businesses and small businesses. It provokes students to question the role of formal rules. You may want to start the discussion by asking, "So, what should the cosmetology board do?" Then you can get some students to defend formal rules and others to argue against them.

ANSWERS TO QUESTIONS

1. *What does this case imply about mechanistic (bureaucratic) organizations?*

    This case implies that mechanistic organizations compel the adherence to rules and procedures without even asking if the rules and procedures should be what they are. In this case, the cosmetology board insists that Taalib obtain a cosmetology license, without considering the hardship on Taalib or the effectiveness of the license, considering that it would have little relevance to his practice.

2. *How would you describe the effectiveness of formulation in the cosmetology board?*

    Formulation in the cosmetology board appears short-sighted. In this case, the board is asserting the formal rules without recognizing that they may not always work. Also, the question remains as to whether they will be carried out. The formulation is of little consequence if the license rule is not enforced.

3. *Build an argument in support of the cosmetology board's reply to "abide by the rules and regulations." Now build an argument against it. Which one of the two arguments do you feel is stronger? Explain.*

    The argument for the reply is that if the board makes an exception here, then it will be faced with numerous potential exceptions. The rule becomes useless if exceptions are always being made. Also, if the license isn't directly relevant, it is bound to teach the cosmetologist general principles and standards, if not specific skills.

The argument against the reply is that formula rules should not be applied at the expense of the people they are supposed to serve. Here, it would seem to serve little purpose for Taalib to get his license. At the same time, the costs would be very great. Arguably, the purpose of the license is to make it more difficult for people like Taalib. With the goal of consistency, these sorts of rules could work against diversity by making it more difficult for people who choose to offer different sorts of services.

CHAPTER 7   ORGANIZATION DESIGN
FOR THE TWENTY-FIRST CENTURY

✓ LECTURE OUTLINE

✓ ANNOTATED OUTLINE

I.   **INTRODUCTION** — p. 151

There are a number of structural options, both organizational and job, at management's disposal.

Notes:

_____

_____

_____

_____

II. **TRADITIONAL ORGANIZATION DESIGNS** — p. 152

When contingency factors support a mechanistic design, there are two options likely to be considered.

A.   The **simple structure** is an organization that is low in complexity and formalization, but high in centralization. It is widely used in small businesses.

1.   Its strengths are its flexibility, speed, and inexpensive cost to maintain.

2.   Its major weakness is that it is effective only in small organizations.

Notes:

_____

_____

_____

_____

B.   The **functional structure** is a design that groups together similar or related occupational specialties.

1.   Its advantage comes from the benefits of specialization.

2.   Its weakness is that the structure does not give managers a broad perspective on organization-wide activities.

Notes:

_____

_____

_____

_____

C. The **divisional structure** is an organization structure made up of autonomous, self-contained units.

   1. Its advantage comes from its self-contained nature and the focus on results.

   2. The drawback is duplication of activities and resources.

   Notes:

   _____

   _____

   _____

   _____

III. **DESIGNS FOR A CHANGING WORLD** — p. 155

   A. The **matrix structure** is a structural design that assigns specialists from functional departments to work on one or more projects that are led by a project manager. A matrix structure creates a dual chain of command.

      1. Its primary strength lies in the grouping of specialists.

      2. Its main weakness is in coordinating the tasks of these specialists.

      Notes:

      _____

      _____

      _____

      _____

   B. The **network structure** is a small centralized organization that relies on other organizations to perform its basic business functions on a contract basis.

      1. It is appropriate for organizations that require very high flexibility.

      2. However, in a network structure, management lacks the close control over operations.

      Notes:

      _____

      _____

      _____

      _____

   C. The **strategic alliance** is a joint partnership between two or more firms that are created to gain a competitive advantage in a market. With globalization, this form is becoming more and more popular.

Notes:

_____

_____

_____

_____

D. An alternative approach is to append an organic structural unit to a mechanistic organization. There are two approaches to doing this.

1. The *task force structure* is a temporary structure created to accomplish a specific, well-defined, complex task that requires the involvement of personnel from other organizational subunits.

2. The *committee structure* is a structure that brings together a range of individuals from across functional lines to deal with problems.

Notes:

_____

_____

_____

_____

E. The **boundaryless organization** is an organizational structure that blurs historic boundaries and increases interdependence among members.

1. The *horizontal structure* is an organizational design option characterized by being flat. Employees are grouped together to accomplish *core processes*.

2. The *vertical structure* is an organizational design option characterized by multilevel teams and empowered employees.

3. The *interorganizational structure* is an organizational design option, such as a strategic alliance, that is characterized by the breaking of classical barriers as separate organizations come together to achieve common ends.

Notes:

_____

_____

_____

_____

IV.   **TQM AND STRUCTURAL DESIGN** — p. 164

Common characteristics of TQM programs often include reduced vertical differentiation, reduced division of labor, and decentralized decision making.

Notes:

_____

_____

_____

V.   **ORGANIZATION CULTURE AND STRUCTURAL DESIGN** — p. 165

An organization has a personality just like individuals do.

A.   **Organizational culture** is a system of shared meaning within an organization that determines, in large degree, how employees act. This definition implies several things.

1.   Culture is a perception that exists in the organization, not in the individual.

2.   Organizational culture is a descriptive term. It describes rather than evaluates.

Notes:

_____

_____

_____

B.   Ten characteristics of an organization's culture have been proposed through research:

1.   Member identity

2.   Group emphasis

3.   People focus

4.   Unit integration

5.   Control

6.   Risk tolerance

7.   Reward criteria

8.   Conflict tolerance

9.   Means-ends orientation

10. Open-systems focus

Notes:

_____

_____

_____

_____

B. The source of culture is usually a reflection of the vision or mission of the organization's founders. It results from the interaction between the founders' biases and assumptions and what the first employees subsequently learned from their own experiences.

Notes:

_____

_____

_____

_____

C. **Strong versus weak cultures**. Strong cultures are characterized by organizations in which the key values are intensely held and widely shared.

1. Whether an organization's culture is strong, weak, or somewhere in between will depend upon organizational factors such as size, age, turnover rate, and intensity of original culture.

2. A culture will have increasing impact on what managers do as it becomes stronger.

Notes:

_____

_____

_____

_____

VI. **JOB DESIGN OPTIONS** — p. 167

The **job characteristics model** (JCM) is a framework for analyzing and designing jobs. It identifies five primary job characteristics, their interrelationships, and impact on outcome variables.

A. There are five **core dimensions** of jobs.

1. *Skill variety* refers to the degree to which a job includes a variety of activities that call for a number of different skills and talents.

2. *Task identity* describes the degree to which a job requires completion of a whole and identifiable piece of work.

3. *Task significance* refers to the degree to which a job has a substantial impact on the lives or work of other people.

4. *Autonomy* describes the degree to which a job provides substantial freedom, independence, and discretion to an individual in scheduling and carrying out his or her work.

5. *Feedback* refers to the degree to which carrying out the work activities required by a job results in an individual's obtaining direct and clear information about the effectiveness of his or her performance.

Notes:

_____ -
_____
_____
_____

B. **Predictions from the model**. To score high on motivating potential, jobs must be high on at least one of the three factors that lead to experiencing meaningfulness. If jobs score high on motivating potential, the model predicts that motivation, performance, and satisfaction will be positively affected.

Notes:

_____
_____
_____
_____

C. **Guides for managers**. The JCM provides specific guidance to managers.

1. *Combine tasks.*

2. *Create natural work units.*

3. *Establish client relationships.*

4. *Expand jobs vertically.*

5. *Open feedback channels.*

   Notes:

   _____
   _____
   _____
   _____

✓ ANSWERS TO REVIEW AND DISCUSSION QUESTIONS

1. *Show how both the functional and matrix structures might create conflict within an organization.*

   The nature of the functional structure focuses each functional unit on its own goals without regard for organizational goals. Since the functions tend to have diverging interests and perspectives, conflict inevitably results and top management must take on the coordination role.

   The nature of the matrix structure has employees report to two sets of managers—along traditional departmental lines and along functional lines. The problem, though, is that this structure often creates confusion and power struggles and thus causes conflict.

2. *What are the strengths and weaknesses of (a) the functional structure and (b) the divisional structure?*

   The main weakness of the functional structure is that the organization tends to focus on functional goals and lose sight of overall organizational goals. Although top management takes on the coordination role, the interplay between functions can result in conflict as each function attempts to assert its own goals. In addition, this structure does not provide adequate training for future senior managers because functional managers are involved in one narrow segment of the organization with only limited exposure to other areas.

   The main weakness of the divisional structure is the duplication of activities and resources that leads to increased organizational costs and reduced efficiency.

3. *Why is the simple structure inadequate in large organizations?*

   The simple structure is inadequate in large organizations because it puts too many demands on top management and fails to take advantage of standardization. As such, it is inefficient and retards competitiveness.

4. *Can an organization have no structure?*

   All organizations have a structure. What may be viewed as no structure is typically a simple structure.

5. *When should management use: (a) the matrix structure, (b) the network structure, or (c) the committee?*

The matrix structure should be used with multiple programs or products and functional departments. The network structure works well for industrial firms that don't want to do their own manufacturing and where reliable suppliers exist. The task force works well with important tasks that have specific time and performance standards that are unique and unfamiliar.

6. *Of the following structural designs—functional, divisional, simple, network, or matrix—which one would you most prefer to work in? Least prefer? Why?*

Student responses to this question will vary. However, most students seem to prefer the simple structure because of its autonomy and minimal degree of formalization. Most typically say they would least like a matrix. This is probably because of its complexity and the confusion created by having multiple bosses.

7. *"What a manager does in terms of the organizing function depends on what level he or she occupies in the organizational hierarchy." Discuss.*

To a large extent, what a manager does in terms of the organizing function depends on what level he or she occupies in the organizational hierarchy. For instance, lower-level managers focus on job design issues and the structure of their departments. The primary issues of organization structure, as discussed in Chapter 10, are typically decided upon by senior-level managers.

8. *Describe the characteristics of a horizontal organizational structure. How do you think "tomorrow's" employees will accept these characteristics?*

A horizontal organizational structure is characterized by being flat and having a reduced number of levels of bureaucracy. They cut across all aspects of the organization and instead of having functional specialties located in departments working on distinctive tasks, they have employees who work together to accomplish core processes.

Since "today's" employees are already accepting such structures, it is likely that "tomorrow's" will as well. In addition, in light of new technology that provides for such things as the virtual corporation, it is possible that horizontal structures will become even more popular.

9. *Contrast job enlargement and job enrichment in terms of the job characteristics model.*

Job enlargement meets the skill variety criterion of the JCM and possibly the task significance criterion. Job enrichment, however, meets the criteria of skill variety, task identity, autonomy, feedback, and possibly task significance.

10. ***Define organizational culture.***

The organizational culture, the "personality of the organization," is the system of shared meaning within an organization that determines, to a large degree, how employees act.

11. ***Contrast organizational culture with formalization.***

Organizational culture is something that loosely and informally suggests how people within an organization are to behave. It tends to encompass things that aren't written down, and that often aren't directly spoken about, such as shared values and rituals. Formalization, on the other hand, refers to the specific, formal rules, polices, and procedures that are usually written down.

12. ***Classrooms have cultures. Describe your class culture. How does it affect your instructor?***

Answers to this question will vary. Have students look at the ten characteristics described in the text chapter and rate the characteristics from high to low for the class. Particular attention should be focused on variables such as individual initiative, direction, control, and conflict tolerance.

✔ SUGGESTIONS FOR DISCUSSING BOXED MATERIAL

Percy Barnevik, CEO of ABB: Although the matrix structure is appropriate for some large, global organizations, is it always the appropriate structure for large, global organizations? Does it matter if the organization hires people who are citizens of the countries where they work or transfers people from other countries?

Do Matrix Structures Create Schizophrenic Employees?: In a matrix structure, it is often the case that employees have to juggle priorities for different managers. Is it the responsibility of managers to deal with their subordinates' potential competing loyalties? If so, how can managers prevent potential conflicts or deal with them as they arise?

J. Richard Hackman and Greg R. Oldham: The Job Characteristics Model: What does the JCM tell us? Should we trust its results?

✓ SUGGESTIONS FOR THE SELF-ASSESSMENT EXERCISE

This assessment exercise is designed to provide the student with his or her propensity for an enriched job. Have students complete the self-assessment and score it. Divide the class into groups by scores: those who have a high growth need (greater than 4.0) and those who have a low growth need (less than 4.0). Then have students answer the following questions:

* Do you feel this score accurately reflects you? Why or why not?

* Have you had jobs in the past that support your score? Explain.

* Why do you desire (or not desire) complex, challenging work?

✓ COMMENTS ON CLASS EXERCISE

The purpose of this exercise is to acquaint students with different types of organizational structures. When the students come back together as a class, ask the students the following questions:

* What type of people would you like to work with in a large organization? Work for?

* What type of people would you like to work with in a small organization? Work for?

* In what type of organization would you manage well? Be a good subordinate?

* What qualities in the culture of the organization where you hope to work are most important?

* Can you think of personal examples where organizational culture has negatively or positively influenced your work or the work of someone you know?

* How can you find out about an organization's culture before you start working there?

✓ ANSWERS TO CASE APPLICATION QUESTIONS

1. ***What role does organization culture play in creating a proper match between employees and their jobs?***

   Because employees spend so much of their time at work, it is important that the organization where they work embrace a culture conducive to their productivity. It is important that employees find a place to work that matches their own preferences regarding such aspects as flexibility, responsibility, and sociability. Otherwise, it is likely that they will not remain content for long and will thus seek a new work environment, even if they are not aware that the problem exists with the culture of the organization.

2. ***How can restructuring the organization affect its culture?***

   Restructuring an organization causes many changes to take place, particularly with regard to responsibility and flexibility. In addition, it influences the types of people the organization attracts.

3. ***If you were Steffen's boss at Kodak, and were pleased with his work, what argument would you build to attempt to keep Steffen from resigning?***

   Steffen has not given the job much time. In addition, he has not expressed concern. Perhaps his manager should consider encouraging Steffen to express his concerns. Then, if the organization did not respond, Steffen should consider leaving. If he expresses his dissatisfaction and explains its causes, though, both he and the organization have the opportunity to benefit.

✓ SUGGESTIONS FOR USING VIDEO CASE

"Just How Strong Can Organizational Culture Be?"

Running Time: 12:59

This video case provides an insightful look into the potentially encompassing nature of organizational culture. While these companies do not necessarily represent the norm, they do provoke thought and discussion.

The video case works well as a conclusion to the chapter. After learning about what organizational culture means, the case causes students to wonder just how much culture should mean. As a conclusion to your discussion of the chapter material, you may want to temper these extreme examples with some less controversial examples.

ANSWERS TO QUESTIONS

1. **Do you believe organizations have the right to hold you accountable for such actions as smoking, drinking, or eating too much junk food off the job? Discuss.**

   In light of the scenarios provided, you should expect many students to respond belligerently that organizations should not have the right to control off-the-job behavior. The fact remains, however, that more and more organizations are holding their employees accountable for their off-the-job behavior, such as by tying health insurance benefits to each employee's health. Other students, though, may argue that what the organization does is its business, as long as employees are warned ahead of time that they will be held accountable for off-the-job behavior.

   Many students would probably be willing to accept the allocation of benefits according to off-the-job behavior. Most objections will probably focus on the penalization of employees for off-the-job behavior, particularly when employees lose their jobs.

2. *Recognizing that both Janice Bone and Daniel Winn understood their organizations' cultures, do you believe that their off-work behavior reflected an unwillingness to accept corporate norms? Explain your position.*

   Expect answers to this question to vary. Some students may argue that the cultures of these organizations inherently included values regarding off-work behavior. If so, then, through their behavior, Janice and Daniel apparently rejected at least some of the corporate norms. Other students may argue that accepting an organization's culture does not mean accepting every value that the culture entails. It is possible to argue that, by adjusting their workplace behavior, Janice and Daniel were accepting corporate norms to the degree with which they were able.

3. ***What effect do such policies, rules, and regulations at both Ford Meter or Best Lock have on creating a strong culture? If the culture in either of these organizations was weak, do you believe either Janice or Daniel would have met the same fate? Explain.***

If enforced regularly, such policies, rules, and regulations have a great impact on the creation of a strong organizational culture. It is not likely that either Janice or Daniel would have experienced the same fate had the cultures of their organizations been weak. Managers could not have justified firing these employees if the values were not widely accepted, because the costs associated with firing—particularly those concerning employee morale—would be too high. In the instances discussed, it appears that the employees were aware of the relevant policies and that most employees willingly accepted the norms.

CHAPTER 8   HUMAN RESOURCE MANAGEMENT

✓ LECTURE OUTLINE

✓ ANNOTATED OUTLINE

I. **INTRODUCTION** — p. 176

The quality of an organization is, to a large degree, determined by the quality of the people who work for the organization. This chapter addresses the issues associated with human resource management.

Notes:

_____

_____

_____

_____

II. **MANAGERS AND HUMAN RESOURCE MANAGEMENT** — p. 177

Whether or not an organization has a personnel department, every manager is involved with human resource decisions.

Notes:

_____

_____

_____

_____

III. **THE HUMAN RESOURCE MANAGEMENT PROCESS** — p. 177

A. **The human resource management process** is defined as activities necessary for staffing the organization and sustaining high employee performance.

Notes:

_____

_____

_____

_____

B. There are nine steps to the human resource management process.

IV. **IMPORTANT ENVIRONMENTAL FACTORS AFFECTING HRM** — p. 178

There are numerous environmental forces that intrude upon human resource management activities.

A. **Federal laws and regulations** have been greatly expanded since the 1960s.

Notes:

_____

_____

_____

_____

B. Exceptions to federal laws and regulations can occur only through **bona fide occupational qualifications** (BFOQ) which are defined as a criterion such as sex, age, or national origin that may be used as a basis for hiring if it can be clearly demonstrated to be job related.

Notes:

_____

_____

_____

_____

C. **Affirmative action programs** are also being used by many organizations. These are programs that enhance the organizational status of members of protected groups.

Notes:

_____

_____

_____

_____

V. **STRATEGIC HUMAN RESOURCE PLANNING** — p. 180

A. How Does an Organization Conduct an Employee Assessment?

Strategic Human resource planning is the process by which management ensures that it has the right personnel, who are capable of completing those tasks that help the organization reach its objectives.

1. Assessment typically takes place through a **human resource inventory**.

2. Another part of the current assessment is the **job analysis** which is an assessment that defines jobs and the behaviors necessary to perform them.

3. From this information, management can draw up a **job description** which is a written statement of what a jobholder does, how it is done, and why it is done.

4. Also, management can develop a **job specification** which is a statement of the minimum acceptable qualifications that an incumbent must possess to perform a given job successfully.

Notes:

_____
_____
_____
_____

B. How future needs are determined involves a determination of future human resource needs by looking at the organization's objectives and strategies.

Notes:

_____
_____
_____
_____

VI. **RECRUITMENT AND SELECTION** — p. 181

A. **Recruitment** is the process of locating, identifying, and attracting capable applicants.

1. *Sources for recruits* are varied and should reflect the following.

   a. Local labor market.

   b. Type or level of position.

   c. Size of the organization.

2. Some sources are superior to others. For example, employee referrals are recognized as superior.

3. *Decruitment* involves the techniques used to reduce the labor supply within an organization.

   Notes:

   _____

   _____

   _____

   _____

B. The **selection process** is the process of screening job applicants to ensure that the most appropriate candidates are hired.

   1. *Reliability* is the ability of a selection device to measure the same thing consistently.

   2. *Validity* describes the proven relationship that exists between a selection device and some relevant criterion.

   Notes:

   _____

   _____

   _____

   _____

C. **Selection devices** are varied and numerous.

   1. *The application form* is used by almost all organizations for job candidates.

   2. *Written tests* can include tests of intelligence, aptitude, ability, and interest.

   3. *Performance simulation tests* involves having job applicants simulate job activities. Two well-known performance simulation tests are as follows:

      a. *Work sampling* is a personnel selection device in which job applicants are presented with a miniature replica of a job and are asked to perform tasks central to that job.

      b. *Assessment centers* are places in which job candidates undergo performance simulation tests that evaluate managerial potential.

   4. *Interviews* are very popular as a selection device, although there are many concerns about the reliability and validity of them.

   5. *Background investigations* can be done in one of two ways:

a.   Verification of application data.

b.   Reference checks.

6.   *Physical examinations* are often used for jobs with physical requirements.

Notes:

_____

_____

_____

_____

D.   Choosing Between Selection Devices

Each selection device has both strengths and weaknesses, and the manager must evaluate each device according to the circumstances at hand.

Notes:

_____

_____

_____

_____

E.   Global Assignments

Careful selection and heightened criteria must be used to screen candidates for global assignments.

Notes:

_____

_____

_____

_____

VII.   **ORIENTATION AND TRAINING** — p. 191

A.   **Orientation** is defined as the introduction of a new employee into his or her job and the organization.

1.   Major objectives of orientation include the following:

a.   Reduce initial anxiety.

b.   Familiarize new employees with the job, the work unit, and the organization.

   c.   Facilitate the outsider-insider transition.

   2.   Management has an obligation to the new employee to insure that the integration of the employee into the organization is as smooth and anxiety-free as possible.

   Notes:

   _____

   _____

   _____

   _____

B.   **Employee training** is a critical component of the human resource management program. There are two different approaches to training.

   1.   *On-the-job training* is extremely common. It can involve job rotation and understudy assignments. It might also involve a mentor or coach relationship.

   2.   *Off-the-job training* can involve classroom lectures, films, and simulation exercises.

   Notes:

   _____

   _____

   _____

   _____

VIII.   **CAREER DEVELOPMENT** — p. 193

Careers are viewed in a variety of ways.

A.   A **career** is defined as a sequence of positions occupied by a person during the course of a lifetime.

Notes:

_____

_____

_____

_____

B. The **career stages model** is the most popular way to view careers.

1. *Exploration* is when individuals are exploring possible career options and making critical choices.

2. *Establishment* begins with the search for work and getting that first job.

3. *Midcareer* is when an individual is no longer seen as a "learner."

4. *Late career* is when an individual can share his or her knowledge with others in the organization.

5. *Decline* is when an individual leaves the work force.

6. *Applying the career stage model* can be of great benefit to managers.

Notes:

_____

_____

_____

_____

IX. **LABOR-MANAGEMENT RELATIONS** — p. 194

Only about 12 percent of the U.S. labor force belongs to a *labor union*, an organization that represents workers and seeks to protect their interests through collective bargaining. *Labor-management relations* is defined as the formal interactions between unions and an organization's management.

A. Good labor-management relations are important because good labor-management relations can produce a number of positive outcomes for management during negotiations.

Notes:

_____

_____

_____

_____

B. The **collective bargaining process** is defined as the process for negotiating a union contract and for administering the contract after it has been negotiated.

1. *Organizing and certification* involve processes that are governed by a federal agency, the National Labor Relations Board.

2. *Preparation for negotiation* is an important step for both parties.

3. *Negotiation* involves proposals and counter-proposals.

4. *Contract administration* is necessary once a contract is agreed upon and ratified.

Notes:

_____

_____

_____

_____

X. **HRM AND WORK FORCE DIVERSITY** — p. 198

The makeup of the workforce is changing and will impact upon recruitment, selection, and orientation/training.

Notes:

_____

_____

_____

_____

✔ ANSWERS TO REVIEW AND DISCUSSION QUESTIONS

1. ***How does HRM affect all managers?***

   Every manager is involved with human resource decisions in his or her unit, whether or not the organization has a personnel department.

2. ***What are the possible sources for finding new employees?***

   Major sources of potential job candidates include internal search, advertisements, employee referrals, public employment agencies, private employment agencies, school placement, and temporary help services.

3. ***Contrast reject and accept error. Which one is most likely to open an employer to charges of discrimination? Why?***

   Reject errors are errors made by rejecting candidates who would later perform successfully on the job. Accept errors are errors made by hiring candidates who would later perform unsuccessfully on the job. Reject errors can open an employer to discrimination charges because if the person could do the job, then the criteria used to reject or select an individual are not valid.

4. ***Why is decruitment now a major concern for managers?***

   Many organizations are being forced to shrink the size of their work force or to restructure their mix of employee skill composition.

5. ***What are the major problems of the interview as a selection device?***

   While a number of problems were cited in the chapter material, it can be generalized that the major problems with interviews are not necessarily the interview, but with the interviewer. The problems then become the use of unstructured interviews, interviewer bias, premature decisions, weighing negative information too heavily, forgetting what was said by the interviewee, etc.

6. ***What is the relationship between selection, recruitment, and job analysis?***

   The relationship is that all three play a vital role in organizing the human resource needs. While each is a separate activity, they are all interrelated. Job analysis starts the process off by defining what a job entails. From the job analysis comes the job descriptions and job specifications, which are used in the recruitment process. While recruiting, a manager will try to fill a vacancy with an individual who has the characteristics needed to successfully perform the job. Selection, then, is made by hiring people who will be successful on the job. All three must use valid criteria.

7. *Do you think there are moral limits as to how far a prospective employer should delve into an applicant's life by means of interviews and tests?*

The law defines the limits by requiring information to be job related. If the information meets the legality test, it is probably also legitimate from a moral perspective.

8. *Identify three skill categories for which organizations do employee training.*

The three skill categories for which organizations do employee training include technical, interpersonal, and problem solving. Technical skills involve basic skills, such as the ability to read, write, do math, as well as job-specific competencies. Interpersonal skills involve the employee's ability to interact effectively with his or her co-workers and boss. Problem-solving skills involve an employee's ability to use logic or reasoning in the problem-solving process.

9. *What is the goal of orientation?*

Orientation is the formal introduction of a new employee to the organization and the job. Its goal is to reduce anxiety by familiarizing the new employee with his surroundings and his co-workers. This will make a new member feel comfortable during the adjustment period. Underlying orientation, then, is to make a new employee feel welcome, so that the money spent hiring the individual is not lost after the first few weeks.

10. *Do you feel that government should be able to influence the HRM process of organizations through legislation and regulations? Support your position.*

Student responses to this question will vary. In fact, this would be an excellent question to set up as a debate with 1/2 of the class supporting government legislation and regulations and the other 1/2 opposing it.

11. *Assuming that management is already responsive to employee needs, do you think that labor unions benefit employees? Support your position.*

Again, student responses to this question will vary depending upon their knowledge of and experience with labor unions. This question also would be an excellent forum for a debate on the advantages and drawbacks of labor unions. Encourage students to think of the advantages and drawbacks from the perspectives of employees, the organization, and the community.

✓ SUGGESTIONS FOR DISCUSSING BOXED MATERIAL

Linda Siddal, Owner, Simply Stated Business Communications: This example emphasizes how often it is possible to turn seemingly bad situations into positive opportunities. Students might be willing to discuss personal experiences.

Is it Wrong to Write a "Creative" Resume?: You may want to open with a discussion of what it takes to write a resume. This is likely to lighten the mood, as students probably share personal "horror stories." Next, you may want to turn the discussion toward what a manager would look for in a resume. As an exercise, you may want to pose a hypothetical, with the students pretending they are managers looking to fill a certain job (with a proposed description). You may then want to pass around sample resumes. Then you can ask students what the resumes suggested about the candidates in light of the specifics of the open position. You may then want to conclude by returning to a discussion of the students' resumes by asking them how, after the previous discussion, they would now change, or refocus, their resumes.

Interviewing Skills: It would be interesting if you could get your hands on films of simulated interviews. These are helpful in focusing the conversations. You could also try to have the students role play, both as interviewers and interviewees. What are the challenges of interviewing? How does that change your behavior as an interviewee?

John P. Wanous and the Realistic Job Preview: What insight does the realistic job preview offer you into the HRM process? You may want to ask students how they would feel about this as a manager. Is it important to share negatives or positives? Or, since applicants often take the negatives more seriously--arguably, too seriously--does this unfairly bias them against the organization?

✓ SUGGESTIONS FOR THE SELF-ASSESSMENT EXERCISE

This self-assessment exercise requires students to examine their own perspectives on what it means to be successful. Many of your students will not have been faced with some of the hard decisions involved with setting personal priorities in terms of career and family. Encourage them to give some thought to their responses to the assessment. Upon completing the assessment, have students score it and then discuss the following:

* Were you surprised at your results? Why or why not?

* What implications does this have for your future career plans?

* Do you think your results would ever change? Why? What would cause it to change?

* What did you learn about yourself from doing this assessment?

✓ COMMENTS ON CLASS EXERCISE

Have the students prepare for the exercise before class. You might ask them to write up a short summary of what they would do to compare with what they decide in small groups during class. In class, divide the students into small groups of four to six students. Ask the groups to decide which employees will be laid off. Suggest that the students consider the following factors.

* Seniority

* Educational background

* Prior experience with the company

* Relationship with other employees

* Age

* Race

* Sex

* Ability to find new position

Which of these factors are appropriate to consider? Which are not? What other factors should be considered?

✓ ANSWERS TO CASE APPLICATION QUESTIONS

1. *Companies offer benefits as a means of attracting and retaining good employees. Should a community have a voice in those benefits offered by the organization? Even if they are counter to the values of a community?*

   Many people believe that companies should not be restricted by community values. However, it is also possible to argue that companies should not be allowed to move into communities and change the values there.

2. *Suppose that unemployment in Williamson County was 20 percent and the area was economically depressed. Do you believe the commissioners' first position not to give Apple the tax break would have been different? Explain.*

   Their position would have depended upon the staunchness of their convictions. It is possible that it would not have made a difference. It is likely, considering the closeness of the vote, that the economic depression might have initially swayed a few more votes in Apple's favor.

"Forced Retirement for Airline Pilots"

Running Time: 13:30

This video case is an interesting look at how federal rules and regulations can impact an industry. The Federal Aviation Administration mandates that commercial airline pilots retire at the age of 60, regardless of an individual's experience, health, or qualifications. The case raises some interesting issues about the role of government regulations and when they hurt or help human resource management practices.

This video case could be used at any point when presenting chapter material. It would be appropriate at the beginning as an introduction to human resource management issues. It would be appropriate in the section on environmental factors where government laws and regulations are discussed. It also would be appropriate as a conclusion to the chapter as a way to illustrate how organizations (and individuals!) have to deal with human resource management issues.

ANSWERS TO QUESTIONS

1. *What are HRM implications of the Age 60 Rule for airlines?*

    The Age 60 Rule has implications for the entire human resource management process. Employee recruitment, selection, training, and career development are some of the areas that would be impacted by this rule.

2. *Design a test or series of tests that would allow airlines to take advantage of pilot experience without compromising safety.*

    Students' responses to this question will vary. However, the tests should probably include some physical components as well as problem solving ability.

3. *How does the Age 60 Rule fit into the career stage model?*

    The Rule appears to fit into the decline stage of the model. Even though pilots are currently "forced" into the decline stage, the Rule represents a situation where the skills and abilities of those individuals are no longer available to the organization.

CHAPTER 9   MANAGING CHANGE AND INNOVATION

✓ LECTURE OUTLINE

✔ ANNOTATED OUTLINE

I.   **INTRODUCTION** — p. 206

Change has always been part of a manager's job. Managing change and innovation are the focus of this chapter.

Notes:

_____

_____

_____

_____

II. **CHANGE** — p. 206

Change is defined as an alteration in people, structure, or technology. Change is ever-present in organizations and cannot be eliminated. Instead, we need to look at the key issues related to managing change.

Notes:

_____

_____

_____

_____

III. **FORCES FOR CHANGE** — p. 207

A. **External forces** that create the need for change come from various sources.

1. The marketplace.

2. Government laws and regulations.

3. Technology.

4. Labor markets.

5. Economic changes.

Notes:

_____

_____

_____

_____

B. **Internal forces** tend to originate mainly from the internal operations of the organization or from the impact of external changes.

   1. Changes in strategy.

   2. Changes in the work force.

   3. New equipment.

   4. Changes in employee attitudes.

   Notes:

   _____

   _____

   _____

   _____

C. The manager may act as a **change agent**, which is defined as people who act as catalysts and manage the change process.

   Notes:

   _____

   _____

   _____

   _____

IV.   **CHANGE PROCESS** — p. 209

   Two very different metaphors can be used to describe the change process.

   A. The **"calm waters" metaphor** characterizes the process of change as being like a ship crossing a calm sea. It is best illustrated by Lewin's 3-step process for change.

1. *Unfreezing* the equilibrium is the first step. This can be accomplished in one of three ways.

   a. *Driving forces*, which direct behavior away from the status quo, can be increased.

   b. *Restraining forces*, which hinder movement from the existing equilibrium, can be decreased.

   c. The two approaches can be *combined*.

2. The next step is to *implement the change* itself.

3. The final step is to *refreeze* the situation.

Notes:

_____

_____

_____

_____

B. The **"white-water rapids" metaphor** describes change that takes place in uncertain and dynamic environments.

Notes:

_____

_____

_____

_____

C. Not every manager faces a world of constant and chaotic change. However, the number of managers who don't face this type of environment is dwindling fast!

Notes:

_____

_____

_____

_____

V. ORGANIZATIONAL CHANGE — p. 212

Organizations can build up inertia that drives them to resist change.

A. Resistance to change can stem from three reasons.

    1. *Uncertainty.*

    2. *Concern over personal loss.*

    3. *Belief that the change is not in the organization's best interests.*

Notes:

_____

_____

_____

_____

B. Six tactics have been proposed for use by managers in dealing with resistance to change.

    1. *Education and communication.*

    2. *Participation.*

    3. *Facilitation and support.*

    4. *Negotiation.*

    5. *Manipulation and cooptation.*

    6. *Coercion.*

Notes:

_____

_____

_____

_____

VI. **CHANGE AND TQM** — p. 214

Our knowledge of change processes can be used to help determine how to effectively implement TQM.

A. *Focusing the change effort.* The change effort can be focused on any of the following.

    1. *Structure.*

2. *Technology*.

3. *People*.

Notes:

_____
_____
_____
_____

B. *Role of the change agent.* Research has shown that the success of the programs depends upon unwavering commitment from the CEO.

Notes:

_____
_____
_____
_____

C. *A philosophical dilemma.* TQM is a commitment to continuous, incremental change. However, for many organizations, incrementalism isn't good enough. In these instances, TQM should probably be the second phase of a two-phase process.

Notes:

_____
_____
_____
_____

VII.   **STIMULATING INNOVATION** — p. 216

Innovation is important to organizational success in the marketplace.

A. **Creativity vs. innovation.** *Creativity* is the ability to combine ideas in a unique way or to make unusual associations between ideas. *Innovation* is defined as the process of taking a creative idea and turning it into a useful product, service, or method of operation.

Notes:

_____

_____

_____

_____

B. **Fostering innovation**. Three sets of variables have been found to stimulate innovation.

   1. *Structural variables* can be summarized as follows.

      a. Organic structures positively influence innovation.

      b. The easy availability of organizational resources provides a critical building block for innovation.

      c. Frequent inter-unit communication helps break down possible barriers to innovation.

   2. *Cultural variables* show that an innovative culture is likely to be characterized by the following:

      a. *Acceptance of ambiguity.*

      b. *Tolerance of the impractical.*

      c. *Low external controls.*

      d. *Tolerance of risk.*

      e. *Tolerance of conflict.*

      f. *Focus on ends rather than means.*

      g. *Open systems focus.*

Notes:

_____

_____

_____

_____

C. **Human resource variables** show that innovative organizations actively promote the training and development of organizational members so that their knowledge remains current, offer employees high job security, and encourage individuals to become champions of change.

Notes:

_____

_____

_____

_____

✓ ANSWERS TO REVIEW AND DISCUSSION QUESTIONS

1. *Why is handling change an integral part of every manager's job?*

   Handling change is part of every manager's job because customers' demands change, government regulations are modified, employees are replaced, and competitors are typically introducing new products or services. The world is not fixed. As changes occur, managers must adapt to them or fail.

2. *What internal and external forces create the need for organizations to change?*

   Examples of external forces that create the need for organizations to change include the marketplace, government laws and regulations, new technologies, labor market fluctuations, and economic changes. Examples of internal forces that create the need for organizations to change include new organizational strategies, changes in the workforce, the introduction of new equipment, and changes in employee attitudes.

3. *Who are change agents?*

   Change agents are persons who act as catalysts and manage the change process.

4. *Do you think that a low-level employee could act as a change catalyst? Explain.*

   If this low-level employee is a low-level manager, then, yes it is possible that he or she could act as a change catalyst, since any *manager* can be a change agent.

5. *Describe Lewin's three-step change process.*

   Lewin's three-step change process encompasses unfreezing, changing, and refreezing. Unfreezing involves identifying what needs to be changed; changing involves making the change; and refreezing involves ensuring commitment and dedication to the change.

6. *Is TQM consistent with the goal of introducing revolutionary change into an organization? Discuss.*

   No, TQM is not consistent with the goal of introducing revolutionary change into an organization since the philosophy of TQM is continuous improvement. However, introducing TQM into an organization could proceed in a two-step process with the continuous improvement activities of TQM being the second phase.

7. *How do creativity and innovation differ? Give an example of each*

Creativity is the ability to combine ideas in an unusual way. An organization is creative when it finds a way to reuse materials. Innovation is the process of turning creative ideas into useful products or services. The pentium chip is an example of an innovative product.

8. *How can an innovative culture make an organization more effective? Could such an innovative culture make an organization less effective? Explain.*

An innovative culture can make an organization more effective by permitting employees to come up with various new ways to cut costs, make profits, provide customer service, develop products/services, etc. For the most part, such an innovative culture won't make the organization less effective, but we must realize current work must be done. Current goals must be met. We can't have all employees being creative or innovative all the time. Otherwise little, if any, work would get done. Thus, there has to be a limit to innovativeness.

9. *How can management foster innovation?*

Management can foster innovation by providing for the characteristics of organizational culture that encourage innovation. The characteristics of organizational culture that encourage innovation include the following: acceptance of ambiguity, tolerance of the impractical, low external controls, tolerance of risk, tolerance of conflict, focus on ends rather than means, and open systems focus.

10. *Can changes occur in an organization without a champion to foster innovation? Explain.*

People come up with new ideas all the time. However, it takes a champion to turn ideas into products and services. It also takes a champion to energize a group of people to come up with new ideas.

✓ <u>Suggestions for Discussing Boxed Material</u>

Coch and French: Resistance to Change: You may want to begin the discussion by asking students what comes to mind when they think of "change." Coch and French identified a need for employee involvement. How do you get employees involved?

Overcoming Resistance to Change: These are very broad suggestions. Ask students for more specific advice. As an option, you may want to pose a hypothetical change situation involving an unwilling employee, and ask students how they would handle it. You may even want to have a group role play in front of the class. Be sure to take into consideration a variety of parties, including the employee, the manager, higher management, and co-workers.

Dave Miller of Lemco Miller Custom Machine Parts: Is videotaping always a good idea? In what other situations might it be a useful device? In what situations might it be counterproductive?

What Would You Do if You Had Details on a Competitor's Trade Secret: You may want to ask students, "What would you do?" This conversation may raise a variety of issues relating to fair and unfair trade practices. What should the rules be?

✓ <u>Suggestions for the Self-Assessment Exercise</u>

This assessment is designed to provide information on a student's aptitude for managing in a turbulent world. After scoring the assessment, have students divide into homogeneous groups based upon scores. Then have them answer the following questions:

* What does this assessment tell you about your desire to manage in a turbulent world?

* Do you agree or disagree with the results? Explain.

* What career implications might this assessment have? Explain.

✓ COMMENTS ON CLASS EXERCISE

The purpose of this assignment is to acquaint students with the challenges of managing change. You may want to have students meet before class so that time in class can be devoted to discussing alternate strategies. Have students consider the following points:

* What does this exercise reveal about the differences between organization structures?

* What are the factors that influence the chosen structure?

* What else should the decision maker keep in mind?

✓ ANSWERS TO CASE APPLICATION QUESTIONS

1. *Relate the calm-waters and white-water-rapids metaphors to the computer industry in the late 1980s. Which of these metaphors applies to Hewlett-Packard? To Wang?*

   Hewlett-Packard approached the computer industry from a white-water-rapids approach. They saw the dynamics of the industry changing and made changes to adapt it. Wang, on the other hand, approached the industry from a calm-waters perspective. They did not sense that the industry was changing as it was.

2. *Contrast Wang's and H-P's culture. How did they influence management's response to a changing environment?*

   Wang's culture can be described as one that was very staid and conservative. They were resistant to change and acted as if the environment they faced was stable. H-P's culture was just the opposite. They embraced change and encouraged their employees to innovate and take risks.

3. *Could the same managerial actions taken at H-P in the late 1980s have worked at Wang? Support your position.*

Student responses to this question may vary. However, remind them that in order for the managerial actions to be effective, the organizational culture has to be receptive to changes. In the case of Wang, the organizational culture would not have been receptive to the types of dramatic changes that H-P instituted.

✓ SUGGESTIONS FOR USING VIDEO CASE

"Daddy Track: Corporate Response to Changing Roles"

Running Time: 6:45

This video case is a good illustration of the types of career challenges faced by employees and organizations. Although many of your students may not yet be at the stage of the family life cycle in which they are contending with children, chances are high that they will face many of the same types of stresses in the future.

Use this video case at the point in the chapter where the topic of employee stress is introduced. Students undoubtedly can relate to the feelings of stress, although their stress usually stems from other than career-family conflicts.

ANSWERS TO QUESTIONS

1. *Is it unrealistic for a company like Microsoft to expect employees to put their careers ahead of their families? Do you think organizations need to change in response to changing family roles and values?*

   Students will probably be found who agree that, yes it is unrealistic for companies like Microsoft to have these expectations, and those who disagree and feel that it is okay for companies to have these expectations. There is no right or wrong answer to this type of dilemma. However, explain to your students that this type of problem is not going to go away. The career-family conflict has always been there but has become more obvious with the escalation of two-career families.

2. *Working long hours is a widely recognized part of Microsoft's culture. Do you think that Microsoft needs to change its culture to meet the needs of family-oriented employees like Jeff Coulter or do you think that workers like Jeff need to change to fit into Microsoft's culture?*

   The answer probably lies with the necessity for the organization and employees to be honest about their expectations. Microsoft should clearly explain to employees the demands (and commensurate rewards, we hope!) of working for it. Workers like Jeff need to be honest about the types of job they will be happiest doing, given the constraints that they have.

3. ***What external and internal forces exist that may cause Microsoft to change how it deals with the commitment to a long work day? What factors exist to support that Microsoft should do nothing?***

Changes in the marketplace may cause Microsoft to change its commitment to a long work day in that both mommy track and daddy track provisions are being stressed by communities. In addition, technology is enabling employees to do more of their work outside of the office. Therefore, while the day may stay long—or get even longer—it may start seeming shorter to co-workers as employees are able to take their work out of the office.

As long as Microsoft continues to thrive and attract capable employees, perhaps the commitment to a long work day should remain intact. It is possible that most of the employees at Microsoft would be working long work days wherever they were.

Part 4

CHAPTER 10   FOUNDATIONS OF BEHAVIOR

✓ <u>**LECTURE OUTLINE**</u>

✓ ANNOTATED OUTLINE

I.   **INTRODUCTION** — p. 225

This chapter looks at a number of factors that influence employee behavior and what the implications are for management practice.

Notes:

_____

_____

_____

_____

II. **EXPLAINING AND PREDICTING BEHAVIOR** — p. 225

Behavior is defined as the actions of people. *Organizational behavior* is the study of the actions of people at work.

A.   **Focus of organizational behavior**. Organizational behavior focuses on two major areas.

1.   *Individual behavior*.

2.   *Group behavior*.

Notes:

_____

_____

_____

_____

B.   **Goals of organizational behavior**. The goals of OB are to *explain* and *predict* behavior.

Notes:

_____

_____

_____

_____

III.   **ATTITUDES** — p. 227

Attitudes are defined as evaluative statements concerning objects, people, or events.

A.   There are **three components of attitudes**.

1.   *Cognitive component* defines the beliefs, opinions, knowledge, or information held by a person.

2.   *Affective component* is the emotional or feeling segment of an attitude.

3.   *Behavioral component* is an intention to behave in a certain way toward someone or something.

Notes:

_____

_____

_____

_____

B.   **Job-related attitudes** include the following.

1.   *Job satisfaction* is a person's general attitude toward his or her job.

2.   *Job involvement* is the degree to which an employee identifies with his or her job, actively participates in it, and considers his or her job performance important to his or her self-worth.

3.   *Organizational commitment* is an employee's orientation toward the organization in terms of his or her loyalty to, identification with, and involvement in the organization.

Notes:

_____

_____

_____

_____

C.   **Attitudes and consistency**. Research has generally shown that people seek consistency among their attitudes and between their attitudes and their behavior.

Notes:

_____

_____

_____

_____

D. **Cognitive dissonance theory** defines *cognitive dissonance* as any incompatibility between two or more attitudes or between behavior and attitudes.

Notes:

_____

_____

_____

_____

E. **Attitude surveys** involve eliciting responses from employees through questionnaires about how they feel about their jobs, work groups, supervisors, and/or the organization.

Notes:

_____

_____

_____

_____

F. **The satisfaction-productivity controversy**. After the Hawthorne Studies, many managers believed that if you kept people happy, they would be productive. A review of the research on this relationship shows if satisfaction does have a positive effect on productivity, that effect is fairly small.

Notes:

_____

_____

_____

_____

G. **Implications for managers**. There is relatively strong evidence that committed and satisfied employees have lower rates of turnover and absenteeism. Also, the belief that making employees happy will make them productive needs to be re-examined.

Notes:

_____

_____

_____

IV. **PERSONALITY** — p. 231

Personality is defined as a combination of psychological traits that classifies a person.

A. **Predicting behavior from personality traits**. Six personality traits have been extensively examined to determine if behavior can be predicted.

1. *Locus of control* can either be internal or external.

2. *Authoritarianism* is defined as a measure of a person's belief that there should be status and power differences among people in organizations.

3. *Machiavellianism* is a measure of the degree to which people are pragmatic, maintain emotional distance, and believe that ends justify means.

4. *Self-esteem* is an individual's degree of like or dislike for him or herself.

5. *Self-monitoring* is a personality trait that measures an individual's ability to adjust his or her behavior to external situational factors.

6. *Risk taking* refers to an individual's willingness to take risks.

Notes:

_____

_____

_____

_____

B. **Matching personalities and jobs**. Efforts have been made to match the proper personalities with the proper jobs.

1. Holland has developed the best documented personality-job fit theory.

2. The key points of this model are that there do appear to be intrinsic differences in personality among individuals, there are different types of jobs, and that people in job environments congruent with their personality types should be more satisfied.

Notes:

_____

_____

_____

_____

C. **Implications for managers**. The major value of a manager understanding personality differences probably lies in employee selection.

Notes:

_____

_____

_____

_____

D. **Personality Traits and National Cultures**. Nationality influences the dominant personality characteristics of people.

Notes:

_____

_____

_____

_____

V. **PERCEPTION** — p. 236

Perception is defined as the process of organizing and interpreting sensory impressions in order to give meaning to the environment.

A. **Factors influencing perception**. A number of factors operate to shape and sometimes distort perception. These factors are found in the following.

1. *The perceiver.*

2. *The target* or object of perception.

3. *The situation* context.

Notes:

_____

_____

_____

_____

B. **Managers judging employees**. People attempt to explain why other people
    behave in certain ways. In arriving at these explanations, people are inevitably
    biased by the assumptions they make about other people's internal states.

    Notes:

    _____

    _____

    _____

    _____

C. **Attribution theory** is a theory used to develop explanations of how we judge
    people differently, depending on the meaning we attribute to a given behavior.
    The determination of the cause of behavior depends upon three factors.

    1. *Distinctiveness* refers to the whether an individual displays a behavior in
        many situations or whether it is particular to one situation.

    2. *Consensus* refers to whether or not everyone who is faced with a similar
        situation responds in the same way with the same behavior.

    3. *Consistency* refers to the congruence in a person's actions.

    Notes:

    _____

    _____

    _____

    _____

D. **Distorting attributions**. There are errors or biases that distort attributions.

1. *Fundamental attribution error* refers to the tendency to underestimate the influence of external factors and overestimate the influence of internal factors when making judgments about the behavior of others.

2. *Self-serving bias* refers to the tendency for individuals to attribute their own successes to internal factors while putting the blame for failures on external factors.

Notes:

_____

_____

_____

_____

E. **Frequently used shortcuts in judging others**. There are five shortcuts we might take in judging others.

1. *Selectivity* refers to the process by which people assimilate certain bits and pieces of what they observe, depending on their interests, background, and attitudes.

2. *Assumed similarity* is the belief that others are like oneself.

3. *Stereotyping* refers to judging a person on the basis of one's perception of a group to which he or she belongs.

4. *Halo effect* refers to a general impression of an individual based on a single characteristic.

Notes:

_____

_____

_____

_____

F. **Implications for managers**. Managers need to recognize that their employees react to perceptions, not reality.

Notes:

_____

_____

_____

_____

VI.   **LEARNING** — p. 240

Learning is defined as any relatively permanent change in behavior that occurs as a result of experience.

A.   **Operant conditioning** is a type of conditioning in which desired voluntary behavior leads to a reward or prevents a punishment.

Notes:

_____

_____

_____

_____

B.   **Social learning theory** says that people can learn through observation and direct experience. Four processes have been found to determine the influence that a model will have on an individual.

1.   *Attentional processes*, which means that people learn from a model only when they recognize and pay attention to its critical features.

2.   *Retention processes*, which means that a model's influence will depend on how well the individual remembers the model's action.

3.   *Motor reproduction processes*, which describes how an individual can perform the modeled activities.

4.   *Reinforcement processes*, which means that individuals will be motivated to exhibit modeled behavior if positive rewards are provided.

Notes:

_____

_____

_____

_____

C. **Shaping** is systematically reinforcing each successive step that moves an individual closer to the desired response. It can be a useful managerial tool. Behavior can be shaped in four ways.

1. *Positive reinforcement* is providing something pleasant after a behavior.

2. *Negative reinforcement* is rewarding a response with the termination or withdrawal of something unpleasant.

3. *Punishment* penalizes undesirable behavior.

4. *Extinction* involves eliminating any reinforcement that is maintaining a behavior.

Notes:

_____
_____
_____
_____

D. **Implications for managers**. Managers can clearly benefit from understanding the learning process.

Notes:

_____
_____
_____
_____

✓ ANSWERS TO REVIEW AND DISCUSSION QUESTIONS

1. *How is an organization like an iceberg? Use the "iceberg metaphor" to describe the field of organizational behavior.*

   An organization is like an iceberg because a lot of informal elements lie beneath the surface and cannot be observed, just like the base of an iceberg lies below the surface beyond visibility. The field of organizational behavior is like an iceberg because there are many behaviors within in organizations that are not visible or known.

2. *What are the three components of an attitude?*

   The three components of an attitude are the cognitive component, the affective component, and the behavioral component.

3. *Clarify how individuals reconcile inconsistencies between attitudes and behaviors.*

   Individuals will take steps to clarify inconsistencies between attitudes and behaviors that they might have. They do this by altering either the attitudes or the behavior or by developing a rationalization for the discrepancy.

4. *What are attitude surveys and how do they help managers?*

   Attitude surveys involve eliciting responses from employees through questionnaires about how they feel about their jobs, work groups, supervisors, and/or the organization. They can help managers by providing information about areas of employee concern.

5. *What behavioral predictions might you make if you knew that an employee had (a) an external locus of control? (b) a high need for achievement? (c) a low Mach score? (d) low self-esteem?*

   Employees with an external locus of control might be less satisfied with their jobs, more alienated from the work setting, and less involved in their jobs. Employees with a high need for achievement could be expected to want challenging and demanding jobs that would push them to achieve even more. Employees with a low Mach score would be overly idealistic, emotional, and concerned about fair and equitable treatment. Employees with low self-esteem would be more susceptible to external influence.

6. *How could you use personality traits to improve employee selection?*

Certain jobs are better filled by individuals with specific personality traits. For example, individuals high on aggression may perform better in sales instead of in accounting.

7. *What factors do you think might create the fundamental attribution error?*

Fundamental attribution error refers to the tendency to underestimate the influence of external factors and overestimate the influence of internal factors when making judgments about the behavior of others. Factors that might create this include past experience that supports this type of judgment and the tendency toward self-serving bias.

8. *Name four different shortcuts used in judging others. What effect does each of these have on perception?*

Selectivity means that people select only bits and pieces of situations. Assumed similarity is the belief that others are like oneself, which can affect perception about what others are like or what others want from their jobs. Stereotyping is judging a person on the basis of one's perception of a group to which he or she belongs. It can distort perceptual judgments. The halo effect is perceiving an individual based on a single characteristic rather than the total package of who that person is.

9. *What is the self-serving bias?*

The self-serving bias is the tendency for individuals to attribute their own successes to internal factors while putting the blame for failure on external factors.

10. *What is social learning theory? What are its implications for managing people at work?*

Social learning theory is the belief that people can learn through observation and direct experience. The implications for managing people is that we can teach people by allowing them to observe and/or directly experience whatever it is we are trying to teach them.

✓ SUGGESTIONS FOR DISCUSSING BOXED MATERIAL

Leon Festinger and Cognitive Dissonance Theory: You can use this material to start a discussion of what sorts of dissonance exist.

Stephanie Dorgan at the Crocodile Cafe: Does riskiness always pay off? You might want to take an informal pool to find out how many are risk averse? Is it better to be risk averse? What are the disadvantages? In what industries is risk aversity valued? In what industries is risk averisty not valued?

Shaping Behavior Skills: How do you feel about shaping? Do you want to shape behavior? Do you want your behavior shaped?

Is Shaping Behavior a Form of Manipulative Control?: The question about whether or not an employee is responsible for his or her actions that are done as a result of the control of the organization is an interesting one that should be explored in class. Is the employee ever not responsible?

✓ SUGGESTIONS FOR THE SELF-ASSESSMENT EXERCISE

This self-assessment exercise is designed to provide students with their locus of control score or how events affect their lives. After scoring, divide the students into three groups—those with high *internal control* scores, those with high *powerful others* scores, and those with high *chance* scores. The groups should answer the following questions:

* How do you feel your locus of control is reflected in your score? Cite examples of how this is so.

* Does your locus of control affect your dealings with the other two groups? Explain.

* What factors/experiences have you encountered to support your score as it is?

* What are the career implications of your score?

✔ COMMENTS ON CLASS EXERCISE

This exercise is designed to get students out of the habit of thinking about how much they will earn. The goal is to have them thinking about the issues that come into play for the manager deciding how much employees will earn. You might consider posing the following additional questions.

* What factors must a manager consider when determining how much an employee will make?

* Should an employee's immediate supervisor determine the employee's pay rate?

* What will the impact of a salary increase be on the employee and the company?

* What will the impact of no salary increase be on the employee and the company?

* What are the different ways in which the manager can approach and handle the situation?

✔ ANSWERS TO CASE APPLICATION QUESTIONS

1. *Research tells us that several factors shape our perception. Using these factors, explain the popularity of the diner with its rich and famous clientele.*

   Factors such as past experiences and expectations shape perceptions. It can be said that the diner remains popular because the rich and famous clientele have run into each other and have received good service there. In addition, the diner has developed a "personality" of its own that the clientele enjoy. Its unusualness adds to its attraction.

2. *Describe how the personality traits listed in Exhibit 10-3 are witnessed in how Bill Fischler runs the diner.*

   In running the diner, Fischler has demonstrating his enterprising nature in his ability to recognize and cater to the desires of his clientele. In addition, he has remained realistic in not aiming for more than he can deliver. His social nature helps as well.

✓ SUGGESTIONS FOR USING VIDEO CASE

"Are There Individual Differences Between Men and Women?"

Running Time: 8:07

This video case should provoke some heated discussion among your students. It provides a provoking look at the differences, perceived and real, between men and women. It turns out that the differences may not be as striking as we all thought.

The video case is probably best used at the end of your presentation on the chapter material. Students will be better able to appreciate some of the comments and concepts being discussed in the video after they have been introduced to the concepts of individual and organizational behavior.

ANSWERS TO QUESTIONS

1. *In what jobs, if any, would gender be relevant to performance variables such as productivity or absenteeism?*

    Students probably will be hard pressed to identify any jobs in which gender would be relevant to performance variables   You might want to play "devil's advocate" and mention some like: police officer, teacher, accountant, CEO, etc. and get students to discuss why gender is not related to performance variables in any of these careers.

2. *"The fact that women have better-honed senses, are less aggressive, and use communication to facilitate connection would suggest that they have superior qualities for managing in the 1990s than do men." Do you agree or disagree with this statement? Support your position.*

    Again, students probably will have pretty strong feelings about this, one way or the other. Be sure that in supporting their opinion, they have thought through the implications of statements they might be using. This question provides an ideal time to review with students what skills and abilities a manager needs to be successful.

3. *How might managing men and women differ in terms of attitudes, personality, perception, and learning? What suggestions would you have for managers to keep in mind to handle those differences?*

The differences in terms of attitudes, personality, perception, and learning can be seen, not just between men and women, but between different men and different women. Our behaviors that we exhibit as a result of our attitudes, personality, perception, and learning are unique to each one of us. This is a good concept for managers to understand and appreciate.

Chapter 11 Understanding Groups and Teams

✓ Lecture Outline

I. **INTRODUCTION** — p. 249

Work groups are a common arrangement within today's business organizations. Work is being restructured around groups in thousands of organizations. Managers need an understanding of group behavior and the concept of teams in order to appreciate what groups can and cannot do within organizations.

Notes:

_____

_____

_____

_____

II. **UNDERSTANDING GROUP BEHAVIOR** — p. 250

Groups exhibit different behavior, more than just the sum total of each group member's individual behavior.

A. **What is a group**? A *group* is defined as two or more interacting and interdependent individuals who come together to achieve particular objectives. *Formal groups* are work groups established by the organization and have designated work assignments and established tasks. *Informal groups* are natural, social formations that appear in the work environment.

Notes:

_____

_____

_____   _____

_____

B. **Why people join groups**. There are six possible reasons why individuals join groups.

1. *Security.*

2. *Status.*

3. *Self-esteem.*

4. *Affiliation.*

5. *Power*.

6. *Goal achievement*.

Notes:

_____

_____

_____

C. **Basic group concepts**. Some basic concepts are necessary for understanding group behavior.

1. *Roles* are sets of behavior patterns expected of individuals occupying given positions in a social unit. *Role conflict* can occur when an individual is confronted by divergent role expectations.

2. *Norms* are acceptable standards shared by group members. Although each group has its own unique set of norms, there are common classes of norms that appear in organizations that focus on effort and performance, dress, and loyalty. Also, because individuals desire acceptance by the groups to which they belong, they are susceptible to conformity pressures.

3. *Status* is a prestige grading, position, or rank within a group. Status systems are an important factor in understanding group behavior.

4. *Group size* can also affect the group's overall behavior. However, the effect depends which outcomes are focused upon.

5. *Group cohesiveness* is the degree to which members are attracted to one another and share the group's goals.

Notes:

_____

_____

_____

_____

III.   **BUILDING REAL TEAMS** — p. 255

Work teams are formal groups made up of interdependent individuals, responsible for attaining goals. Organizations are increasingly designing work around teams rather than individuals.

A. **Why use a team**? There are a number of reasons why a team will be used.

1. *Creates esprit de corps.*

2. *Allows management to think strategically.*

3. *Speeds decisions.*

4. *Facilitates work-force diversity.*

5. *Increases performance.*

Notes:

_____

_____

_____

_____

_____

B. **Characteristics of effective teams**. There are eight characteristics associated with effective teams.

1. *Clear goals.*

2. *Relevant skills.*

3. *Mutual trust.*

4. *Unified commitment.*

5. *Good communication.*

6. *Negotiating skills.*

7. *Appropriate leadership.*

8. *Internal and external support.*

Notes:

_____

_____

_____

_____

C. **Management challenges**. In spite of the many advantages that teams can usher in, it is not always easy to implement teams.

1. *Obstacles to Team Effectiveness.* Teams need direction and require that members be able to cooperate. Trust is also necessary.

2. *Overcoming Obstacles.* Managers can overcome obstacles by clearly designating the team's purpose, making sure ample resources are available, building mutual trust, and changing team membership when necessary.

Notes:

_____

_____

_____

_____

IV. **TEAMS AND TQM** — p. 263

Teams and TQM. Teams are a central characteristic of TQM.

A. Since the essence of TQM is process improvement, employee participation is critical.

Notes:

_____

_____

_____

_____

B. Another application to TQM is *quality circles*, which are work groups that meet regularly to discuss, investigate, and correct quality problems.

Notes:

_____

_____

_____

_____

✓ ANSWERS TO REVIEW AND DISCUSSION QUESTIONS

1. *How can joining a group increase an individual's sense of power?*

   Joining a group can help increase an individual's sense of power since often what cannot be achieved individually becomes possible through group action. Also, informal groups provide additional opportunities for individuals to exercise power over others.

2. *How might organizations create role conflicts for an employee?*

   Organizations might create role conflicts for employees because of unrealistic expectations. They may require behaviors that aren't natural for the employee or that are at odds with the individual's attitudes.

3. *Identify five roles you play. What behaviors do they require? Are any of these roles in conflict? If so, in what way? How do you resolve these conflicts?*

   Student responses to this question will vary. Some possible roles that they might identify include: student, employee, spouse, son/daughter, boyfriend/girlfriend, fraternity/ sorority member, etc. Be sure that students focus on answering the remaining questions associated with role behaviors. Especially focus on how they resolve any conflicts that might arise.

4. *What is the relationship between a work group and the organization of which it is a part?*

   The work group is a subsystem embedded in the larger organizational system. Since formal groups are subsets of a larger organization, part of the explanation of the group's behavior can be explained by looking at the organization to which it belongs.

5. *What is the most effective size for a group?*

   The most effective size for a group depends upon the focus of the outcomes. Large groups, those with twelve or more members, are good for gaining diverse input. Smaller groups are better at doing something productive with those facts. Groups of approximately seven members tend to be more effective for taking action.

6. *What is the relationship between group cohesiveness and group effectiveness?*

Effectiveness should increase if cohesiveness is high and group/organization goals align. If alignment between group and organizational goals is low and cohesiveness is high, effectiveness likely will decrease.

7. *Why are some groups more successful than others?*

Some groups are more successful than others because they have favorable external conditions; ample internal resources; roles, norms, and leaders that support the group's goals; and positive synergy.

8. *When might individuals, acting independently, outperform teams in an organizations?*

Individuals might outperform teams in an organization when tasks are simple and independent. Simple tasks are routine and standardized. Independent tasks do not rely on others to be completed.

9. *How do you explain the rapidly increasing popularity of work teams in the United States when American culture places such high value on individualism?*

Work teams appear to be rapidly increasing in popularity because of the impact they have on higher productivity, improved quality, and increased employee motivation and satisfaction.

10. *In what ways can the obstacles to effective teams be overcome?*

Managers can overcome obstacles by clearly designating the team's purpose, making sure ample resources are available, building mutual trust, and changing team membership when necessary.

11. *How do you think scientific management theorists would react to the increased reliance on teams in organizations? How about the behavioral science theorists?*

Scientific management theorists would react negatively to the use of teams in organizations. Scientific management focuses on the "one best way" for an individual to do his or her job, and teams would not be conducive to finding this approach. Behavior scientists, on the other hand, probably would be favorable to the idea of teams in organizations. Since teams help focus more challenge and responsibility on individuals, the behavioralists would be in favor of this approach.

✓ SUGGESTIONS FOR DISCUSSING BOXED MATERIAL

Solomon Asch and Group Conformity: Open the conversation up to a variety of groups, such as groups of friends, athletic teams, and organizations. How does desire to be accepted influence behavior? How can managers encourage individuals not to fall into the tendency to conform?

Roger Blitz at Pridemark Custom Homes: What factors most influenced the success of teams at Pridemark? Was the solution the only possible one? Why did teams work here? Was it more than mere luck?

Building Trust Among Team Members: In a competitive situation, trust is often difficult to foster. How can managers encourage trust among team members, without removing incentives for each member to perform at his or her optimal level? Also, how is it possible to be fair?

Should Managers Agree with their Boss when they Don't?: There is a tradeoff between cohesiveness and creativity sometimes. What does a manager do if he or she disagrees with a superior? What sort of message does he or she convey to subordinates and co-workers? Is it possible for an organization to make it possible for employees not to have to unethically conform, without jeopardizing commitment to the organization?

✓ SUGGESTIONS FOR THE SELF-ASSESSMENT EXERCISE

This self-assessment exercise focuses on each student's trustworthiness. Since the results of this exercise would be quite personally sensitive, we recommend that individual scores are kept confidential. After students have taken the exercise and scored it, have them write out answers to the following questions. Emphasize to them that these will not be handed in, but rather used to learn something about themselves.

* What did your results show? How do you feel about these results? Do you think they accurately reflect your trustworthiness? Why or why not?

* Why is trustworthiness important for a manager? (This question could be discussed in class.)

*   What could I do to improve my level of trustworthiness? (Again, this question could be discussed in class.)

✓ COMMENTS ON CLASS EXERCISE

While all of these exercises emphasizes teamwork, this one, in particular, has the students work together in teams to accomplish a specific end. You may want to take a second day to discuss the results of the endeavor. You can then divide the class into small groups. You should separate the students into different teams than the ones they were in on the first day. Ideally, no students who were on the same team on the first day would be on the same team on the second day. On the second day, the teams could discuss the team performance from the first day.

*   Did leaders emerge? If so, how?

*   How did non-leaders feel? Did some people feel that they performed better and were more comfortable as non-leaders?

*   What sort of obstacles were overcome and how?

*   Was group size an issue? Would there have been an ideal size?

*   Would anyone have preferred to work alone? Why?

*   Should the students have chosen the groups or should they have been randomly assigned?

✓ ANSWERS TO CASE APPLICATION QUESTIONS

1. *If you were on one of these GROWTH teams, do you think it would increase or decrease your job satisfaction? Why? Do you think you'd be more productive as a team member than as part of a traditional manufacturing process? Explain.*

In the students' responses look for their recognition of certain issues, such as whether the change is by their choice or imposed upon them. Also, are adequate rewards in place and are the teams supported by the organization as a whole? Or, in the alternative, does it merely translate into more work?

2. ***Under what conditions would the introduction of teams possibly fail and lead to lower group performance in a manufacturing setting?***

When teams are imposed upon workers without adequate communication and compensation, teams can fail, particularly when associated with more work. In addition, certain elements must be present, such as adequate resources and mutual trust. In addition, teams fail when they aren't necessary, such as when the work is independent by nature.

3. ***"Here's a classic example of management responding to the latest fad. Achieving ambitious goals without adding people, equipment, or space is impossible. Continuous improvement cannot create miracles." Do you agree or disagree with this criticism? Discuss.***

Continuous improvement does not create miracles. However, when an organization makes a total commitment to quality and takes the steps necessary to realize it, continuous improvement can achieve results. Goals do not inherently entail adding resources. However, if resources are what is lacking, then continuous improvement will not achieve results if the organization is not willing to supply the resources.

✓ SUGGESTIONS FOR USING VIDEO CASE

"Miracle on 39th Street: The City Pride Story"

Running Time: 5:00

This video case offers an uplifting look into how people can turn misfortune into fortune. There is a lot of talk about downsizing and retrenchment, but little talk of what's next for those people involved. Here is an account of what happened to a group of unemployed workers.

This video case works well with the chapter, and can even be used as an introduction to the chapter. As an introduction, it emphasizes the type of teamwork where people come together naturally because they realize that everyone needs each other and that each team member has something different to offer. You might want to have students think of other such teams that are created voluntarily for similar reasons.

ANSWERS TO QUESTIONS

1. *Based on the group concepts you learned in this chapter, why do you think teams are successful in general? Why do you think the team of fifty individuals at City Pride started this business?*

   Teams are successful when people are willing to make compromises and cooperate. Teamwork takes work. In other words, people have to invest effort in making the team work as well as in doing the assigned work. These individuals started the business as a source of income. They worked together because they recognized that their worth was greater if they combined efforts.

2. *What effect did group cohesiveness have on the workers at City Pride? Cite examples for the case.*

   Willingness to work together and mutual trust was import to this group. Their cohesiveness was integral. It enabled them to stick it out through the difficulties in raising initial funding and through the first salary-less years.

3. *If you were in a similar situation as those Braun Bakery employees, what would you do? Why? Discuss.*

Answers should include a discussion of alternatives as well as the advantages and disadvantages of trusting the group and risking money and effort.

CHAPTER 12   MOTIVATING EMPLOYEES

✓ LECTURE OUTLINE

✓ <u>**ANNOTATED OUTLINE**</u>

I.   **INTRODUCTION** — p. 270

Managers need to know about motivational concepts and practices in order to encourage their employees to make a maximum effort.

Notes:

_____

_____

_____

_____

II.   **MOTIVATION AND INDIVIDUAL NEEDS** — p. 271

Motivation is defined as the willingness to exert high levels of effort to reach organizational goals, conditioned by the effort's ability to satisfy some individual need. A *need* is an internal state that makes certain outcomes appear attractive.

Notes:

_____

_____

_____

_____

III. **EARLY THEORIES OF MOTIVATION** — p. 272

Three specific theories were formulated during the 1950s. Although these theories have been heavily attacked and questions have been raised about their validity, they still provide some strong explanations for employee motivation.

A. **Hierarchy of needs theory** is a theory developed by Abraham Maslow. It states that there is a hierarchy of five human needs. As each need is substantially satisfied, the next need becomes dominant. The five needs are:

1. *Physiological* needs include food, drink, shelter, sexual satisfaction, and other bodily requirements.

2. *Safety* needs include security and protection from physical and emotional harm.

3. *Social* needs include affection, belonging, acceptance, and friendship.

4. *Esteem* needs include internal esteem factors and external esteem factors.

5. *Self-actualization* needs include growth, achieving one's potential, and self-fulfillment.

6. *Lower-level* needs include the physiological and safety needs.

7. *Higher-level* needs include social, esteem, and self-actualization needs.

Notes:

_____

_____

_____

_____

B. **Theory X and Theory Y** were developed by Douglas McGregor and described two distinct views of human nature.

1. *Theory X* was the assumption that employees dislike work, are lazy, seek to avoid responsibility, and must be coerced to perform.

2. *Theory Y* was the assumption that employees are creative, seek responsibility, and can exercise self-direction.

Notes:

_____

_____

_____

_____

C. **Motivation-hygiene theory** is the theory developed by Frederick Herzberg. The theory suggests that intrinsic factors are related to job satisfaction, while extrinsic factors are associated with dissatisfaction.

1. *Hygiene factors* are factors that eliminated dissatisfaction.

2. *Motivators* are factors that increased job satisfaction.

3. Herzberg's theory is not without its criticisms, which were associated with the statistical techniques used in his study.

4. Even with criticisms, Herzberg's theory is widely popular with managers.

Notes:

_____

_____

_____

_____

IV. **CONTEMPORARY THEORIES OF MOTIVATION** — p. 276

The contemporary theories of motivation have a reasonable degree of valid supporting documentation.

A. The **three-needs theory** developed by David McClelland cites the needs for achievement, power, and affiliation as major motives in work.

1. *Need for achievement (n Ach)* is defined as the drive to excel; to achieve in relation to a set of standards; to strive to succeed.

2. *Need for power (n Pow)* is defined as the need to make others behave in a way that they would not have behaved otherwise.

3. *Need for affiliation (n Aff)* is defined as the desire for friendly and close interpersonal relationships.

Notes:

_____

_____

_____

_____

B. **Equity theory** is the theory that an employee compares his or her job's inputs/outcomes ratio to that of relevant others and then corrects any inequity.

1. The *referents* are the persons, systems, or selves against which individuals compare themselves to assess equity.

2. Equity theory recognizes that individuals are concerned with their absolute rewards as well as the relationship of these rewards to what others receive.

3. The theory establishes four propositions relative to inequitable pay.

a. *Given payment by time, over-rewarded employees will produce more than equitably paid employees.*

    b.   *Given payment by quantity of production, over-rewarded employees will produce fewer, but higher-quality units than equitably paid employees.*

    c.   *Given payment by time, under-rewarded employees will produce less or poorer-quality output.*

    d.   *Given payment by quantity of production, under-rewarded employees will produce a large number of low-quality units in comparison with equitably paid employees.*

Notes:

_____

_____

_____

_____

C.   **Expectancy theory** is the theory that an individual tends to act in a certain way based on the expectation that the act will be followed by a given outcome and on the attractiveness of that outcome to the individual. Three relationships are important to this theory.

1.   *Effort-performance linkage*, which is the probability perceived by the individual that exerting a given amount of effort will lead to performance.

2.   *Performance-reward linkage*, which is the degree to which the individual believes that performing at a particular level will lead to the attainment of a desired outcome.

3.   *Attractiveness*, which is the importance that the individual places on the potential outcome or reward that can be achieved on the job.

4.   There are four steps inherent in the theory.

    a.   What perceived outcomes does the job offer the employees?

    b.   How attractive do employees consider these outcomes to be?

    c.   What behavior must employees exhibit to achieve these outcomes?

    d.   How do the employees view their chances of doing what is asked?

Notes:

_____

_____

_____

_____

D. **Integrating contemporary theories of motivation**. Figure 16.7 presents a model that integrates much of what is known about motivation.

1. The basic foundation is the simplified expectancy model.

2. The model also considers the achievement-need, reinforcement, and equity theories.

3. Rewards also play an important role in the model.

Notes:

_____

_____

_____

_____

E. **Transferability of theories of motivation across national cultures**. Many of these theories apply to other countries, particularly Western industrialized countries.

Notes:

_____

_____

_____

_____

V. **MOTIVATING A DIVERSIFIED WORK FORCE** — p. 286

To maximize motivation among today's diversified work force, managers need to think in terms of being flexible.

Notes:

_____

_____

_____

_____

✓ ANSWERS TO REVIEW AND DISCUSSION QUESTIONS

1. *What role do needs play in motivation?*

   A need is an internal state that makes certain outcomes appear attractive. An unsatisfied need creates tension that stimulates drives within an individual. Motivated individuals are in a state of tension and to relieve this tension, they exert effort. This tension-reduction effort should be directed at organizational goals.

2. *What role would money play in (a) the hierarchy of needs theory, (b) motivation-hygiene theory, (c) equity theory, (d) expectancy theory, and (e) employees with a high n Ach rating?*

   (a) Money meets lower order needs. (b) Money is a hygiene factor. (c) Money is an outcome that people compare. (d) Money may be one reward that has value to the employee. (e) Not relevant, since high achieving individuals are intrinsically motivated.

3. *Contrast lower-order and higher-order needs in Maslow's need hierarchy.*

   Lower-order needs include the physiological and safety needs. These needs are satisfied externally. Higher-order needs include the social, esteem, and self-actualization needs. These needs are satisfied internally.

4. *If you accept Theory Y assumptions, how would you be likely to motivate employees?*

   A manager who accepted Theory Y assumptions would likely motivate employees through participation in decision making, responsible and challenging jobs, and good group relations.

5. *Describe the three needs in the three-needs theory.*

   David McClelland's three-needs theory proposed the following: need for achievement, which is the drive to excel, to achieve in relation to a set of standards, to strive to succeed; need for power which is the need to make others behave in a way that they would not have behaved otherwise; and need for affiliation which is the desire for friendly and close interpersonal relationships.

6. *Would an individual with a high n Ach be a good candidate for a management position? Explain.*

High achievers typically don't make good managers. They want to do things themselves. They don't have a lot of faith in others and have difficult delegating. High achievers understand driving themselves, but not working through others.

7. *What are some of the possible consequences of employees perceiving an inequity between their inputs and outcomes?*

Employees can (1) distort either their own or others' inputs or outcomes, (2) behave in some way to induce others to change their inputs or outcomes, (3) behave in some way to change their own inputs or outcomes, (4) choose a different comparison chart, or (5) quit their jobs.

8. *What difficulties do you think work force diversity causes managers trying to use equity theory?*

Work force diversity would cause managers difficulty with trying to meet the needs of a variety of individuals. Under equity theory, individuals compare their ratio of inputs/outcomes to that of a referent. In a diverse work force, these referents could be inappropriate comparisons. To maximize motivation among today's diversified workers, managers need to think in terms of being flexible.

9. *What role does perception play in (a) expectancy theory, (b) equity theory, and (c) reinforcement theory?*

Expectancy theory—the strength of a tendency to act in a certain manner depends on the strength of the perceived outcome.

Equity theory—perception determines equity or inequity between inputs and outcome.

Reinforcement theory—this does not depend on perception, but on the actual reward for a certain behavior.

10. *Explain the motivation implications of expectancy theory for management practice.*

The key to expectancy theory is understanding an individual's goal, the linkage between effort and performance, between performance and rewards, and between rewards and individual goal satisfaction. The expectancy theory recognizes that there is no universal principle for explaining everyone's motivation.

✓ SUGGESTIONS FOR DISCUSSING BOXED MATERIAL

David McClelland and the Three-Needs Theory: What does it mean for business if the best managers are high in the need for power and low in the need for affiliation? What else do McClelland's results mean for business?

The Ethics of CEO Compensation: Who is responsible for the high salaries many CEOs receive? Is it ethical for people like Eisner to make exorbitant sums, more than a person could dream about spending in a lifetime? What is the justification for such extremely high CEO salaries? If we wanted to change this, how could we?

Getting the Most from Employees: How could a manager motivate you? Would any of the suggested principles work? Would you feel comfortable applying the principles suggested? What else could you do? How much time should a manager dedicate to motivating his or her employees?

Nancy Singer of First of America Bank: Here is another example of how minorities and women are making a difference in the business world. Does the Golden Rule always work?

✓ SUGGESTIONS FOR THE SELF-ASSESSMENT EXERCISE

This self-assessment exercise is designed to force students to identify the needs that are most important to them. Again, this type of exercise might be perceived as delving into personally sensitive areas. Therefore, you would probably want to have students complete and score the exercise on their own. Then, ask your students to answer the following questions:

* What does your scoring on this exercise tell you?

* Were you surprised by your scores? Why or why not?

* What career implications can you obtain from this self-assessment?

* Do you think that your scores on this self-assessment could change in the future? Why or why not?

✓ COMMENTS ON CLASS EXERCISE

The purpose of this exercise is to introduce students to the challenges of motivating employees. After everyone has completed the exercise, have students consider the following:

* What sort of motivators exist?

* What sort of disparities exist between what motivates individuals and what managers think motivates individuals?

* How should motivation techniques change according to the size of the organization?

* How does a manager motivate a diverse workforce comprised of numerous individuals who respond to different motivators?

✓ ANSWERS TO CASE APPLICATION QUESTIONS

1. *Describe the behavior (stealing) of these employees in terms of (a) hierarchy of needs, (b) motivation hygiene theory, (c) equity theory, and (d) expectancy theory.*

   According to the hierarchy of needs, since the organization was not fulfilling basic needs (i.e., job security), workers were concerned with basic needs (physiological) and their ability to continue to feed their families and did not feel compelled to continue living by the rules.

   According to motivation hygiene theory, the organization was lacking hygiene factors and this caused prevalent job dissatisfaction. The level of job satisfaction was not entirely relevant, according to this theory, because job dissatisfaction and job satisfaction can coexist, and as long as job dissatisfaction exists, negative behavior can result.

According to equity theory, these employees must have felt that they were not getting enough from the organization compared to other employees at similar organizations. They thus decided to *take* what the organization was not *giving*.

According to expectancy theory, these employees must have thought that, since they weren't being rewarded for good behavior, they wouldn't be punished for bad behavior either. In addition, the stealing must have seemed attractive considering the decreased pay.

2. *What could management have done differently to avert this "potential" problem?*

Management could have communicated better about what was going on. In addition, management could have considered making concessions, such as shorter work weeks or improved conditions. Management could have worked with employees to reach a mutually beneficial solution.

✓ SUGGESTIONS FOR USING VIDEO CASE

"Amdahl Corporation"

Running Time: 4:48

This video case is especially interesting considering the tremendous amount of downsizing that has taken place. You may want to begin by asking if any students have participated in programs such as Outward Bound. If so, what sort of memories do they have, particularly of the people they participated with?

As an introduction to the chapter, you can then use it to refer back to as you discuss the various theories. For example, you can talk about what needs are fulfilled and how this activity outside the workplace translates into the workplace. As a conclusion to the chapter, it is an interesting example of how companies recognize the need to pay attention to motivation. In addition, it ties in nicely to the next chapter on teamwork.

ANSWERS TO QUESTIONS

1. *Explain how downsizing affects the motivation process for those laid off? For the survivors?*

   People who lose their jobs often suffer from inevitable demoralization. Even though the primary reason is the economy, they often cannot help wondering why it was them and not the others. Their motivation to work is weakened, as is their self-confidence in looking for new jobs. They often doubt their own abilities as well as the possibility of vacancies elsewhere. Survivors suffer from missing their co-workers and having to do their work in addition to their own. In addition, they often lack motivation because they wonder how long it will be before their turn comes.

2. *How can a training program in the wilderness, which helps individuals overcome their fears of heights, be applicable to an organization's environment?*

   Fear is an emotion that can hinder a person in activities from sports to work. By learning to handle emotions such as fear, employees can learn to be productive workers in the present without always worrying about the future. In addition, it exposes workers to "the bigger picture" of what life is about. Perhaps most important, by supporting such endeavors, the organization encourages employees to continue standing together and supporting each other.

3. ***Explain the wilderness training in terms of expectancy theory. How can such a program affect individual goals?***

According to this theory, the wilderness training demonstrates to employees that just because some employees are laid off, it doesn't mean that the organization doesn't support its employees. To the contrary, it says that if employees remain motivated, the organization will prosper and employees will probably be able to keep their jobs. The goal is to encourage hope. As long as employees retain hope, they will remain motivated to achieve what they can. In addition, such wilderness training can serve to invigorate employees to aim for individual objectives.

CHAPTER 13   LEADERSHIP AND SUPERVISION

✓ LECTURE OUTLINE

✓ ANNOTATED OUTLINE

I.   **INTRODUCTION** — p. 294

Leadership is important in organizations because leaders are the ones who make things happen.

Notes:

_____

_____

_____

_____

II.   **MANAGERS VS. LEADERS** — p. 294

There are distinctions between the two classifications. Managers are appointed and have legitimate power within the organization. *Leaders* are those who are able to influence others and who possess managerial authority.

Notes:

_____

_____

_____

_____

III.   **TRAIT THEORIES** — p. 295

The *trait theories* of leadership are those theories isolating characteristics that differentiate leaders from nonleaders.

A.   Finding a set of **consistent and unique personality traits** that could apply across the board to all effective leaders has been impossible.

Notes:

_____

_____

_____

_____

B. However, attempts to identify traits **consistently associated with leadership** have been more successful. In fact, six traits on which leaders seem to differ from nonleaders have been isolated.

1. Drive

2. The desire to lead

3. Honesty/integrity

4. Self-confidence

5. Cognitive ability

6. Knowledge of the business

Notes:

_____

_____

_____

_____

IV. **BEHAVIORAL THEORIES** — p. 296

Since the trait theories did not provide any solid clues to effective leaders, researchers began to examine the behaviors specific leaders exhibited. The *behavioral theories* are the theories identifying behaviors that differentiate effective from ineffective leaders. Two of the most popular studies will be described next.

A. The **Ohio State studies** conducted in the late 1940s sought to identify independent dimensions of leader behavior. The researchers found two categories that accounted for most of the leadership behavior.

1. *Initiating structure* is the extent to which a leader defines and structures his or her role and those of subordinates to attain goals.

2. *Consideration* is the extent to which a person has job relationships characterized by mutual trust, respect for subordinates' ideas, and regard for their feelings.

3. The studies also proposed that a *high-high leader*, one who was high in both initiating structure and consideration, achieved high subordinate performance and satisfaction more frequently.

Notes:

_____

_____

_____

_____

B. The **University of Michigan studies** were being done about the same time as the Ohio State studies and had similar research objectives. These researchers also came up with two dimensions of leadership behavior.

   1. Leaders who were *employee oriented* were described as emphasizing interpersonal relations, taking a personal interest in subordinates' needs, and accepting of individual differences.

   2. Leaders who were *production oriented* emphasized the technical or task aspects of the job. They were concerned mainly with accomplishing the group's tasks and regarded group members as a means to that end.

Notes:

_____

_____

_____

_____

C. **The managerial grid** is a two-dimensional portrayal of leadership based on concerns for people and for production.

   1. It was developed by Blake and Mouton and has nine possible positions on the grid.

   2. The five key positions identified by Blake and Mouton were as follows.

      a. *1,1 Impoverished*

      b. *9,1 Task*

      c. *1,9 Country-club*

      d. *5,5 Middle-of-the-road*

      e. *9,9 Team*

   3. Blake and Mouton concluded that managers perform best using a 9,9 style.

Notes:

_____

_____

_____

_____

D. **Behavior theories and leadership.** Consistent relationships between patterns of leadership behavior and successful performance could not be identified. Instead, researchers began to recognize the need to look at situational factors.

Notes:

_____

_____

_____

_____

V. **CONTINGENCY THEORIES OF LEADERSHIP** — p. 300

The contingency theories of leadership attempt to identify key situational variables that determine the effectiveness of a leadership situation.

A. **The Fiedler model** was the theory developed by Fred Fiedler. The theory states that effective groups depend upon a proper match between a leader's style of interacting with subordinates and the degree to which the situation gives control and influence to the leader.

   1. Fiedler developed the *least-preferred co-worker (LPC) questionnaire* that measured whether a person is task- or relationship-oriented.

   2. He also isolated three situation criteria that he believed could be manipulated to create the proper match with the behavioral orientation of the leader. These three are as follows:

      a. *Leader-member relations* is the degree of confidence, trust, and respect subordinates have in their leader.

      b. *Task structure* is the degree to which the job assignments are made according to set procedures.

      c. *Position power* is the degree of influence a leader has over power variables such as hiring, firing, discipline, promotions, and salary increases.

3. The next step was to evaluate the situation in terms of these three contingency variables. Fiedler defined eight different situations in which a leader could find himself or herself.

4. The Fiedler model proposes matching an individual's LPC and an assessment of the three contingency variables to achieve maximum leadership effectiveness.

5. Fiedler concluded that task-oriented leaders tend to perform better in situations that were very favorable or very unfavorable to them.

6. He also concluded that relationship-oriented leaders perform better in moderately favorable situations.

Notes:

_____

_____

_____

_____

B. **Path-goal theory**, which is the theory that a leader's behavior is acceptable to subordinates insofar as they view it as a source of either immediate or future satisfaction.

1. The essence of the theory is that it is the leader's job to assist his or her followers in attaining their goals and to provide the necessary direction and support to ensure that their goals are compatible with organizational goals.

2. Four leadership behaviors were identified by House as part of the model.

   a. The *directive leader* lets subordinates know what is expected of them, schedules work to be done, and gives specific guidance on how to accomplish tasks.

   b. The *supportive leader* is friendly and shows concern for subordinates' needs.

   c. The *participative leader* consults with subordinates and uses their suggestions before making a decision.

   d. The *achievement-oriented leader* sets challenging goals and expects subordinates to perform at their highest level.

3. The path-goal theory proposes two classes of situational or contingency variables that moderate the leadership behavior-outcome relationship.

a. The ones in the *environment* are outside the control of the subordinate.

b. Those that are part of the *personal characteristics of the subordinate*.

Notes:

_____

_____

_____

_____

C. **Leader-participation model** is a leadership theory developed by Vroom and Yetton that provides a set of rules to determine the form and amount of participative decision making in different situations.

1. The model assumes that any of five behaviors may be feasible in a given situation.

   a. *Autocratic I (AI)*

   b. *Autocratic II (AII)*

   c. *Consultative I (CI)*

   d. *Consultative II (CII)*

   e. *Group II (GII)*

2. Vroom and Jago have revised the model to include twelve contingency variables as well as the five alternative leadership styles.

3. The leader-participation model confirms that leadership research should be directed at the situation rather than at the person.

Notes:

_____

_____

_____

_____

D. **Sometimes leadership is irrelevant**! Leadership may not always be important. Numerous studies indicate that, in many situations, any behaviors a leader exhibits are irrelevant.

Notes:

_____

_____

_____

_____

VI.   **EMERGING APPROACHES TO LEADERSHIP** — p. 306

Two approaches to leadership have emerged from recent studies.

A.   **Charismatic leadership** theory is an extension of attribution theory and suggests that followers make attributions of heroic or extraordinary leadership abilities when they observe certain behaviors.

   1.   Three personal characteristics of charismatic leaders have been identified.

      a.   Extremely high confidence.

      b.   Dominance.

      c.   Strong convictions in his or her beliefs.

   2.   An increasing amount of research shows impressive correlations between charismatic leadership and high performance and satisfaction among followers.

   3.   Most experts think that individuals can be trained to exhibit charismatic behaviors.

   4.   Charismatic leadership may not always be needed to achieve high levels of employee performance. It may be most appropriate when an employee's job has a lot of ideological content.

   Notes:

   _____

   _____

   _____

   _____

B.   **Transactional versus transformational leadership.** *Transactional leaders* are leaders who guide or motivate their followers in the direction of established goals by clarifying role and task requirements. *Transformational leaders* are leaders who provide individualized consideration, intellectual stimulation, and possess charisma.

Notes:

_____

_____

_____

_____

VII.   **FIRST-LINE SUPERVISION** — p. 308

A.   The **supervisor** completes the job of directing immediate activities of employees.

Notes:

_____

_____

_____

_____

B.   The supervisor's job is unique primarily because the supervisor does not direct the activities of other managers.

Notes:

_____

_____

_____

_____

C.   The supervisor's role is different in that managers differ with regard to how integral they perceive that role. It is a difficult position because they are not considered staff by staff or managers by managers.

Notes:

_____

_____

_____

_____

D. The supervisor's role is changing through the influence of technology and the emphasis on boundaryless organizations.

Notes:

_____

_____

_____

_____

✓ ANSWERS TO REVIEW AND DISCUSSION QUESTIONS

1. **"All managers should be leaders, but not all leaders should be managers." Do you agree or disagree with this statement? Support your position.**

   Management and leadership are two different things. Managers are appointed. They thus have legitimate power to reward and punish. The sources of their power are formal. Leaders, on the other hand, may be appointed, or they can emerge independently from within a group. Their influence can extend beyond the bounds of formal authority.

   The fact that someone can lead does not mean that he or she is capable of handling the interpersonal relations and logistics of managing. On the other hand, ideally, if someone is in a management role—one where he or she is positioned so as to be observed by subordinates—it is valuable for him or her to be able to influence others to act beyond the dictates of formal authority.

2. **Discuss the strengths and weaknesses of the trait theory of leadership.**

   The trait theory of leadership isolates certain characteristics that supposedly identify leaders. Six traits have been identified that leaders often share, but this theory is not enough to explain leadership because it doesn't take situational factors into account.

3. **What is the managerial grid? Contrast its approach to leadership with that of the Ohio State and Michigan groups.**

   The managerial grid, developed by Blake and Mouton, is a graphic portrayal of a two dimensional view of leadership style. It has nine positions on each axis. One axis is concern for people. The other is concern for production. The managerial grid is dimensionally similar to both Ohio State and Michigan group studies as shown by the following chart:

Managerial Grid	OSU	Michigan
Concern for people	Consideration	Employee-oriented
Concern for production	Initiating structure	Task-oriented

4. **Is "high-high" the most effective leadership style? Explain.**

Certainly, a "high-high" leadership style has been shown to achieve high productivity and high job satisfaction, but one must realize in what situations. Although it can generate positive outcomes, it must be viewed from a situational approach.

5. *What similarities, if any, can you find among all the behavioral theories?*

The behavioral theories were similar in that all identified the two dimensions of leadership behavior: task and people. Each of the theories had its own name for the dimensions but the dimensions themselves were present. Also, the behavioral theories were similar in that all were missing consideration of the situational factors that influence success or failure.

6. *How is a least-preferred coworker determined? What is the importance of one's LPC for the Fiedler theory of leadership?*

According to the Fiedler theory of leadership, a least-preferred coworker is determined by using the least-preferred coworker questionnaire which measures whether a person is task or relationship oriented. The scale is significant in that Fielder's model proposes that it is important to have a proper match between the leader's style and the degree to which the situation gives the leader control and influence. This is dictated by the type of employees who are present.

7. *What are the contingencies in the path-goal theory of leadership?*

The two contingencies are the variables in the environment that fall outside the control of the subordinate, such as task structure, the formal authority system, and the work group, and those that are part of the personal characteristics of the subordinate, such as locus of control, experience, and perceived ability.

8. *What is charismatic leadership? Can people learn to be charismatic leaders? Explain.*

Charismatic leaders are those who exhibit heroic characteristics. Charismatic leadership occurs when followers attribute heroic or extraordinary leadership qualities to people when they observe certain behaviors. Most experts believe that individuals can be trained to exhibit charismatic behaviors. For example students in one research study were trained to articulate an overriding goal, communicate high-performance expectations, exhibit confidence in the ability of followers to meet these expectations, and empathize with their subordinates' needs.

9. *"Charismatic leadership is always appropriate in organizations."* **Do you agree or disagree? Support your position.**

No, charisma may not always be appropriate in organizations. It appears to be most appropriate where employees' jobs have an ideological component. In fact, charismatic leaders may become a liability to an organization once a crisis has been resolved and the need for dramatic change lessens.

10. *Contrast transactional and transformational leaders.*

Transactional leaders guide their followers toward goals by clarifying role and task requirements. Transformational leaders inspire followers to reach beyond their own self-interests for the good of the organization.

11. *What is a first-line supervisor? Why is that job unique in management?*

A first line supervisor is the first level of management whose task is to direct the activities of immediate employees. The position is unique in that it is key to getting the work done, but it is neither staff nor management.

12. *"First-line supervision will become tomorrow's dinosaur. With the rapid changes in American businesses, there will be little need for supervisors for tomorrow's organizations." Do you agree or disagree with this statement? Explain.*

Expect answers to focus on the rise of empowerment, electronics and the virtual workplace, and TQM. With such movements toward lack of supervision, it is likely that the statement is at least somewhat true.

✓ SUGGESTIONS FOR DISCUSSING BOXED MATERIAL

James G. Kaiser at Corning Inc.: Most managers appear to believe that they have to make decisions or take credit for making decisions in order to receive praise. Kaiser demonstrates that this is not true. What are some of the qualities that seem to make Kaiser great? Who are some other successful African-Americans?

Fred Fiedler and the Fiedler Contingency Model of Leadership: Fiedler has made an important contribution to understanding leadership effectiveness. Why? Does it make sense to you? Nevertheless, there are problems with the model. What are they?

Is it Unethical to Create Charisma: The traditional view is that charisma is a quality that a select few people naturally have. Do you agree? Name some people you consider charismatic. Why would charisma be important? At the same time, some people argue that, with all the image-building that the media does, it is possible to create charismatic images. Do you believe this is true? If so, how could that be done? Is there anything unethical about creating images of charisma?

Coaching Skills: When is coaching necessary? Is it possible to coach more than one person at the same time? What skills do you recommend? What skills do you respond to best? What skills do the authors not mention?

✓ SUGGESTIONS FOR THE SELF-ASSESSMENT EXERCISE

This self-assessment exercise focuses on leadership behavior, which in turn, influences the type of leader one is or would be. Have students complete the instrument and score it. Then divide them into three groups: those most likely to exhibit autocratic, shared, or laissez-faire styles of leadership. Within these homogeneous groups, have students answer the following questions:

* Cite examples of how you use this predominant style effectively.

* How does this leadership style work **for** you?

* How does this leadership style **get in your way**?

* What insights does this leadership assessment provide for you?

✓ COMMENTS ON CLASS EXERCISE

This exercise is aimed at getting students to compare intuition and theory. MAKE SURE STUDENTS COMPLETE THE EXERCISE BEFORE READING THE CHAPTER. In class, have students consider the following:

* Were there many similarities between the characteristics identified prior to reading the chapter and after?

* Are there characteristics that intuition indicates that the theories do not? Are there characteristics that theories indicate that intuition do not? How do you explain the differences?

* Think about the good leaders you know. Which characteristics do they exhibit?

* What does this exercise tell you about leadership characteristics?

✓ ANSWERS TO CASE APPLICATION QUESTIONS

1. *What critical factors will influence Sue's success as a leader? Would these factors be the same if success were defined as group satisfaction rather than group productivity?*

   The main factors that will influence Sue's success as a leader will be those established by the organization. Namely, in this department, Sue will be measured by productivity—getting policy renewals out on time, processing them properly, etc. If group satisfaction was defined as the goal, there might be some change, as the emphasis would be more people-oriented as opposed to task-oriented goals.

2. *Do you think that Sue can choose a leadership style? If so, describe the style you think would be most effective for her. If not, why?*

Sue needs to choose a leadership style that best fits her. She would be wise to choose a style that allows for participation/input from her employees. A situational leadership theory would be appropriate here because of the diverse range in maturity of her employees. She could also fall back upon the path-goal theory and choose to behave according to characteristics that match the demands of the environment and her subordinates.

3. *What suggestions might you make to Sue to help her win over or control Lillian Lantz?*

Sue must view Lillian as an asset, not a liability. She should get as much information from Lillian as possible. Lillian could be the key to Sue's success. Accordingly, Sue needs to ensure that Lillian's needs are being met.

"Evan Kemp of the EEOC"

Running Time: 5:06

This video case provides an inspiring look into the business world. Kemp demonstrates that people are not limited in their accomplishments. He has been described as a bold risk taker, brash, confident, and a self-promoter. He is also a man with big ideas. And he is in a wheel chair. Furthermore, in addition to his own success, Kemp has made possible the success of other people with similar problems. This case works well as a conclusion to the chapter, opposite Ted Turner as the introduction.

ANSWERS TO QUESTIONS

1. *Contrast the leadership style of Ted Turner and Evan Kemp. Why do you think both are successful?*

   Both are men with great ideas who see opportunities where others are blind. The primary difference between the two styles appears to be that Kemp has had to fight harder. His style is characterized by overcoming barriers, whereas Turner's style is characterized by doing what no one else dreamed of before. Both are successful because they are creative, they persevere, and they don't give up.

2. *Would you call Kemp's leadership style charismatic? Describe the aspects of Kemp's leadership philosophy that make that philosophy work.*

   Whether or not Kemp is to be considered charismatic depends upon whether it is believed that he has behaved extraordinarily. His philosophy works because he doesn't give up. Moreover, he is willing to show people why they are wrong—i.e., explain the financial benefits of hiring the handicapped—instead of just saying they are wrong because they are wrong.

3. *Who would you rather work for—Ted Turner or Evan Kemp? Why?*

   Turner is a visionary, but it is not clear how he treats his employees. Kemp, though, appears to have a personal agenda. Expect answers to vary.

CHAPTER 14 COMMUNICATION AND CONFLICT MANAGEMENT

✓ **LECTURE OUTLINE**

✓ ANNOTATED OUTLINE

I.   **INTRODUCTION** — p. 320

Communication is fundamentally linked to managerial performance. Understanding the role and functions of communication within an organization is important to managers.

Notes:

_____

_____

_____

_____

II.   **UNDERSTANDING COMMUNICATION** — p. 321

Everything a manager does involves communication. The importance of effective communication for managers cannot be overemphasized. Managers need effective communication skills.

A.   **Communication** is defined as the transferring and understanding of meaning. This chapter focuses on *interpersonal communication* which is communication between two or more people in which the parties are treated as individuals rather than objects.

Notes:

_____

_____

_____

_____

B.   **The communication process** is made up of seven stages.

1.   The *communication source*

2.   The *message*, defined as a purpose to be conveyed

3.   *Encoding*, defined as converting a message into symbols

4.   The *channel*, the medium by which a message travels

5.   *Decoding*, which is retranslating a sender's message

6. The *receiver*

7. *Feedback*

8. The entire process is susceptible to *noise*, which is disturbances that interfere with the transmission of a message.

Notes:

_____
_____
_____
_____

C. **Methods of communicating**. Four popular methods of communicating will be described next.

1. *Oral* communication, or talking, is the method most people use to communicate with each other.

    a. The advantages are quick transmission and quick feedback.

    b. The major disadvantage is the potential for distortion.

2. *Written* communication is using any device that transmits written words or symbols.

    a. The advantages include having a record of the communication and the attention that is given to writing a message.

    b. The drawbacks are that it takes more time and the lack of feedback.

3. *Nonverbal communication* which is communication transmitted without words. It typically includes the following:

    a. *Body language* which refers to gestures, facial configurations, and other movements of the body that convey meaning.

    b. *Verbal intonation* which is an emphasis given to words or phrases that conveys meaning.

4. *Electronic media* which includes the sophisticated technology available to carry our communications. It includes such techniques as the telephone, fax machines, and closed-circuit television. The fastest growing may be *electronic mail* which is instantaneous transmission of written messages on computers that are linked together.

_____

_____

_____

_____

D. **Barriers to effective communication** include the general distortions of the communication process as well as the following:

1. *Filtering,* which is the deliberate manipulation of information to make it appear more favorable to the receiver.

2. *Selective perception,* whereby the receiver selectively sees and hears communications depending on his or her needs, motivations, experience, and other personal characteristics.

3. *Emotions,* which describe how the receiver feels when a message is received.

4. *Language* can be a problem since words mean different things to different people.

5. *Nonverbal cues* can be a barrier if the oral communication and the nonverbal communication are incongruent.

Notes:

_____

_____

_____

_____

E. **Overcoming the barriers.** Managers can overcome the barriers by using some of the following suggestions.

1. *Use feedback*

2. *Simplify language*

3. *Listen actively*

4. *Constrain emotions*

5. *Watch nonverbal cues*

Notes:

_____

_____

_____

_____

III. CROSS-CULTURAL INSIGHTS INTO COMMUNICATION PROCESSES — p. 330

Interpersonal communication is conducted differently depending on the culture in which it is taking place. Managers need to account for cultural differences when attempting to communicate with diverse employees.

Notes:

_____

_____

_____

_____

IV. CONFLICT MANAGEMENT SKILLS — p. 332

Managers also need the ability to manage conflict.

A. **What is conflict**? *Conflict* is perceived incompatible differences that result in interference or opposition. There are three different views of organizational conflict.

1. The *traditional view of conflict* is the view that all conflict is bad and must be avoided.

2. The *human relations view of conflict* is the view that conflict is a natural and inevitable outcome in any organization.

3. The *interactionist view of conflict* is the view that some conflict is necessary for an organization to perform effectively.

Notes:

_____

_____

_____

_____

B. **Functional versus dysfunctional conflict**. The interactionist view of conflict does not suggest that **all** conflicts are good. *Functional conflicts* are conflicts that support an organization's goals. *Dysfunctional conflicts* are ones that prevent an organization from achieving its goals.

Notes:

_____

_____

_____

_____

C. **Developing effective conflict resolutions skills** involves following these suggestions.

1. Know your underlying conflict-handling style.

2. Be judicious in selecting the conflicts that you want to handle.

3. Evaluate the conflict players.

4. Assess the source of the conflict.

5. Know your options.

   a. *Avoidance* is withdrawal from or suppression of conflict.

   b. *Accommodation* is resolving conflicts by placing another's needs and concerns above one's own.

   c. *Forcing* is satisfying one's own needs at the expense of another's.

   d. *Compromise* is a solution to conflict in which each party gives up something of value.

   e. *Collaboration* is resolving conflict by seeking a solution advantageous to all parties.

Notes:

_____

_____

_____

_____

D. **Conflict stimulation**. The thought of stimulating conflict is frightening to most managers. However, there are some situations in which conflict must be stimulated. The following suggestions are provided.

1. Change the organization's culture.

2. Use communication.

3. Bring in outsiders.

4. Restructure the organization.

5. Appoint a devil's advocate, a person who purposely presents arguments that run counter to those proposed by the majority.

Notes:

_____

_____

_____

_____

✓ ANSWERS TO REVIEW AND DISCUSSION QUESTIONS

1. *Why isn't effective communication synonymous with agreement?*

   Effective communication requires only understanding, not agreement. Many people confuse the two, however.

2. *Where in the communication process is distortion likely to occur?*

   Distortion can occur any place in the communication process. No stage in the process is exempt from potential distortion.

3. *"Ineffective communication is the fault of the sender." Do you agree or disagree with this statement? Support your position.*

   Disagree. It may be the sender's fault, but it may also be due to the receiver's lack of attention, the channel chosen, the lack of feedback, etc. Any point within the communication process is potentially a cause of ineffective communication.

4. *What are the most popular communication methods used by people in organizations?*

   The most popular communication methods used by people in organizations are verbal interaction, written communications, nonverbal communication, and electronic media.

5. *Why are effective interpersonal skills so important to a manager's success?*

   Managers, by definition, get things done through other people. Regardless of how good they are at planning, organizing, making decision, etc., if they can't communicate and work effectively with people, they will suboptimize their performance.

6. *What is conflict?*

   Conflict is the perceived incompatible differences that result in interference or opposition.

7. *Contrast the traditional, human-relations, and interactionist views of conflict.*

   The traditional view of conflict seeks to eliminate all conflict. The human-relations view accepts conflict. The interactionist view recognizes the value of conflict, its importance to keeping the organization responsive and innovative, and the occasional need to stimulate conflict when conflict levels are too low.

8. *What view of conflict—traditional, human-relations, or interactionist—do you think most managers have? Do you think this view is appropriate?*

Most managers accept the traditional view of conflict because they think conflict is bad and disruptive. Most organizational cultures reward managers for minimizing conflicts; therefore, most managers emphasize "keeping the peace" regardless of the cost.

9. *What are the five primary conflict-resolution techniques?*

The five primary conflict-resolution techniques are avoidance, accommodation, forcing, compromise, and collaboration.

10. *Why would a manager ever want to stimulate conflict?*

A manager would want to stimulate conflict in several situations: (1) the manager is surrounded by "yes people," (2) employees are afraid to admit ignorance and uncertainties to the manager, (3) the decision makers are so focused on compromise that they lose sight of values, long-term objectives, or the organization's welfare, (4) managers believe they should maintain the appearance of peace and cooperation, regardless of the cost, (5) the decision makers are too afraid of hurting employees' feelings, (6) managers are more concerned with employees' popularity than with their competence and high performance, (7) managers are overly interested in obtaining consensus for their decisions, (8) employees appear excessively resistant to change, (9) there is a lack of new ideas, and (10) there is low employee turnover.

✓ SUGGESTIONS FOR DISCUSSING BOXED MATERIAL

Tom Colesberry at Ruiz Foods Products: Ruiz takes pains to communicate with the members of his organization. Has he gone too far? Has he gone far enough? Should American companies compensate for employees who speak languages other than English? What else could Colesberry do? What type of information do you believe Colesberry receives from one-on-one conversations? Is there a way he could receive more balanced, more accurate information?

Is it Unethical to Purposely Distort Information: How important is information to employees? How much information are employees entitled to? Is it wrong to tell lies to employees? "White lies"? To withhold the truth? Are there ever circumstances where it is o.k. for managers not to tell the truth to employees? Under what sort of circumstances might it be reasonable?

Developing Effective Active Listening Skills?: Are you a good listener? What are your strongest listening skills? What skills are important to you in your listeners? You may want to try a short exercise and have students practice talking and listening with one another. Have the listeners alternate between being good listeners and being bad listeners. Ask students to talk about how it affects what they say and why.

Kenneth W. Thomas and Conflict-Handling Techniques: Which technique do you prefer? Why? Have you ever tried another technique? How would knowing an opponent's preferred technique influence your interactions with him or her?

✓ SUGGESTIONS FOR THE SELF-ASSESSMENT EXERCISE

This self-assessment exercise is designed to show students what conflict handling style they favor. Have students complete the assessment and the scoring. Then, you could divide them into groups to work on the following questions or work on the questions individually.

* What did your score tell you about your conflict handling style?

* Were you surprised by your results? Why or why not?

* How could this information help you as a manager?

* Do you think your style might change? Why or why not?

✓ COMMENTS ON CLASS EXERCISE

The purpose of this exercise is to encourage students to practice using good active listening skills. Here are the answers to the questions:

Club Name: Short Snout Society

    Purpose: To improve porcine/pig image (or give them the needed love and affection)

    Founder: Jack Tate

    Place: Greenville, S.C.

    When: March, 1984

    Membership: 350 members in 8 states and 3 foreign countries

    Cost to Join: $50

    Tate's Score: 21 out of 30

    Money Raised: $25,000

    Tate's Job: Runs a chain of 20 infant-apparel stores

✓ ANSWERS TO CASE APPLICATION QUESTIONS

1. *Analyze how hold jockeys at WP help to enhance communication between the company and customers.*

   Hold jockeys make the "holding" more personal. In addition, the system provides "holders" with information. At the same time, it communicates the underlying message that WP cares about the people holding and wants to make the wait easier.

2. *Considering that the electronic media is the "wave of the future," what potential barriers for effective communications does this create?*

   People today already get frustrated by the electronic communications they must weed through. Many people still want a voice. While an organization can anticipate most problems, there are always a few that will fall between the cracks.

3. *"Efforts at companies like WordPerfect, Lotus, and Microsoft to hire hold jockeys are reversing a trend in telephone customer service operations—going from automated systems back to people-run operations." Do you agree or disagree with this statement? Support your position.*

While the hold system seems more user-friendly, it is an appearance, not a reality, because this system does not replace electronic answer-giving in many situations. This is an option in some cases, but many organizations will inevitably continue to automate because it's more efficient.

✓ SUGGESTIONS FOR USING VIDEO CASE

"Kansas City Police Chief Steven Bishop"

Running Time: 5:19

This video case is a good example of how important communication is in our everyday lives *and* in our careers. Given the news media popularity of the Rodney King incident, this case meshes well with illustrating what consequences, both positive and negative, communication can have.

This case probably is best used at the end of the chapter material since students would benefit by an understanding of the communication process and interpersonal skills as they watch the video. Show the video after you have lectured over all of the chapter material and then discuss the case questions in class.

ANSWERS TO QUESTIONS

1. *Describe how police officers can use nonverbal communication to intimidate citizens.*

   Nonverbal communication can be used by police officers to intimidate citizens by the demeanor they exhibit and the language they use. Even the "tools of the trade," (i.e. gun, mace, riot stick, etc.) can be intimidating if the officer is handling them as if he or she is preparing to use them.

2. *How are effective interpersonal skills necessary for the cop on the beat? For a police chief?*

   Effective interpersonal skills are necessary for the cop on the beat since he or she is dealing first-hand and close-up with citizens. Also, the police officer is often called upon in tense, upsetting situations where it is particularly important to be able to listen, negotiate, and communicate. Interpersonal skills also are necessary for a police chief since this individual constantly is in the public's eye. It is important that a person in this position exhibit good interpersonal skills and serve as a good role model for the police officers on the line.

3. *Chief Bishop believes you can teach improved communication skills to police officers. Others say that the selection process and group norms in these jobs work against open, sensitive communication with citizens. What do you think?*

Student responses to this question will vary. You hope that most will agree that these skills can be taught although students do need to recognize that the situations faced by police officers are unique and tense. In many of these situations, interpersonal skills will not make a difference in outcome.

Part 5

CHAPTER 15   FOUNDATIONS OF CONTROLLING

✓ **LECTURE OUTLINE**

✓ ANNOTATED OUTLINE

I.   **INTRODUCTION** — p. 345

Regardless of the thoroughness of the planning, an idea still may be poorly or properly implemented without a satisfactory control system.

Notes:

_____

_____

_____

_____

II. **CONTROL** — p. 345

Control is the process of monitoring activities to ensure they are being accomplished as planned and of correcting any significant deviations.

Notes:

_____

_____

_____

_____

III.   **IMPORTANCE OF CONTROL** — p. 346

Control is important since it serves as the final link in the functional chain of management.

Notes:

_____

_____

_____

_____

IV.   **CONTROL PROCESS** — p. 346

The *control process* is the process of measuring actual performance, comparing it against a standard, and taking managerial action to correct deviations or inadequate standards.

A.   **Measuring** is the first step in the control process.

1.   *How we measure* can be shown by four common sources of information that managers use.

a.   Personal observation

b.   Statistical reports

c.   Oral reports

d.   Written reports

2.   *What we measure* is probably more critical than the how. Both objective and subjective measures are used.

Notes:

_____

_____

_____

_____

B.   **Comparing** is the next step in the control process, and it determines the degree of variation between actual performance and the standard. It is critical to determine the *range of variation*, which is the acceptable parameters of variance between actual performance and the standard.

Notes:

_____

_____

_____

_____

C.   **Taking managerial action** is the final step in the control process. Although the manager might decide to "do nothing," two other alternatives are possible.

1.   *Correct actual performance.* Once the manager has decided to correct actual performance, he or she has another decision to make.

      a.   Take *immediate corrective action*, which is correcting an activity at once in order to get performance back on track.

      b.   Take *basic corrective action*, which is determining how and why performance has deviated and correcting the source of deviations.

      c.   The action taken will depend upon the cost/benefit of doing so.

2.   *Revise the standard.* If the standard was set too high or too low, a manager may decide to revise it.

Notes:

_____

_____

_____

_____

V.   **TYPES OF CONTROL** — p. 351

There are three basic types of control.

A.   **Feedforward control** is control that prevents anticipated problems.

Notes:

_____

_____

_____

_____

B.   **Concurrent control** is control that occurs while an activity is in progress.

Notes:

_____

_____

_____

_____

C.   **Feedback control** is control that is imposed after an action has occurred.

VI. **QUALITIES OF AN EFFECTIVE CONTROL SYSTEM** — p. 354

Ten characteristics are identified as qualities that effective control systems tend to have in common.

A. Accuracy — p. 354

B. Timeliness — p. 354

C. Economy — p. 354

D. Flexibility — p. 354

E. Understandability — p. 354

F. Reasonable Criteria — p. 354

G. Strategic Placement — p. 354

H. Emphasis on the Exception — p. 355

I. Multiple Criteria — p. 356

J. Corrective Action — p. 356

VII. **CONTINGENCY FACTORS OF CONTROL** — p. 357

Several situational factors influence the effectiveness of control systems.

A. Organizational Size

B. Position and Level

C.   Degree of Decentralization

D.   Organizational Culture

E.   Importance of an Activity

Notes:

_____

_____

_____

_____

VIII.   **ADJUSTING CONTROLS FOR NATIONAL DIFFERENCES** — p. 359

Managers must make sure and take account of the impact of culture on controlling in such ways as the degree of control, impact of technology, and constraints on corrective action.

Notes:

_____

_____

_____

_____

IX.   **DYSFUNCTIONAL SIDE OF CONTROLS** — p. 359

Controls also can have a dysfunctional side. When controls are inflexible or control standards are unreasonable, people lose sight of the organization's overall goals. Also, people can engage in behaviors designed to influence the information system that is gathering data during a given control period. Keep in mind that controls have both positive aspects and negative aspects.

Notes:

_____

_____

_____

_____

✓ ANSWERS TO REVIEW AND DISCUSSION QUESTIONS

1. ***What is the role of control in management?***

   The role of control in management is to monitor the activities to ensure they are being accomplished as planned, and to correct any significant deviations.

2. ***How are planning and control linked?***

   The control process assumes that standards exist already. These existing standards are established in the planning function.

3. ***In Chapter 9 we discussed the white-water view of change. Do you think it's possible to establish and maintain effective standards and controls in this type of atmosphere? Explain.***

   It is absolutely essential for organizations to establish and maintain effective standards and controls in this type of environment of rapid change. The control system would need to be flexible and clearly focused on the important measures.

4. ***Why is what is measured probably more crucial to the control process than how it is measured?***

   The criteria that are measured become the focus of attention. Whatever criteria are chosen, people will emphasize and attempt to look good on that criteria.

5. ***Name four methods managers can use to acquire information about actual performance.***

   The four methods are personal observation, statistical reports, oral reports, and written reports.

6. ***Contrast immediate and corrective action.***

   Immediate action deals with the problem on its surface. It addresses the outcome and not the cause. Corrective action looks for the cause of the problem and corrects it. The latter is more difficult to do than the former.

7. *What are the advantages and disadvantages of feedback control?*

Feedback control provides managers with meaningful information about how effective the planning effort was. Feedback can also enhance employee motivation. However, it is after the fact. It tends to be more costly because it fails to anticipate problems.

8. *Why is feedforward control the most popular type of control?*

Feedforward control is the most popular type of control because it is future-directed and prevents problems from happening.

9. *What can management do to reduce the dysfunctionality of controls?*

Since controls have both a positive side and a negative side, managers need to design flexibility into the control system in order to reduce the dysfunctionality of controls. By being flexible, managers can hopefully avoid some of the problems associated with strict controls.

10. *Do you think goal setting and TQM programs facilitate the control process? Explain your answer.*

Goal setting and TQM programs probably do facilitate the control process since both are very specific in terms of what the standards are and what is important to be measured. For example, under a goal setting program, such as an MBO program, the objectives that are participatively-established by the subordinate and the superior would be the standards against which performance is measured. Under a TQM program, where the goal is continuous improvement, standards would be established to ensure that this goal is being met and monitored.

✓ SUGGESTIONS FOR DISCUSSING BOXED MATERIAL

Providing Feedback: Why is feedback valuable? How often should it be given? Should only the manager offer feedback, or can coworkers also provide useful feedback? Can or should an employee request feedback? What advice would you give a manager offering you positive feedback? What advice would you give a manager offering you negative feedback? What advice would you give an employee receiving feedback from you?

Betty Smith of Mr. Sweeper Stores, Inc.: Is automation always the answer to how to increase control? When might automation be a bad idea? What else could Smith have done?

Control and Employees' Right to Privacy: Where does a manager draw the line between control and privacy? Should a manager have a say in how employees behave outside work? How much control should they be able to exercise in the workplace? Should an organization be allowed to pry into the personal affairs of employees', such as by monitoring phone calls and social affairs, for the sake of the organization? What if unfair competition is suspected, such as the disclosure of trade secrets?

✓ SUGGESTIONS FOR THE SELF-ASSESSMENT EXERCISE

This self-assessment exercise focuses on students' willingness to delegate. Have students complete the assessment and score it. After scoring, divide the students into two homogeneous groups: those with scores between 18-53 and those with scores between 54-90. In these groups, have students answer the following questions:

* Why do you believe you are an effective/ineffective delegator? Can you cite some examples of how you delegate?

* How does this effectiveness/ineffectiveness affect your managerial ability?

* Why do you delegate? *or* Why don't you delegate?

* How could you change your approach?

✓ COMMENTS ON CLASS EXERCISE

This exercise is aimed at getting students to integrate planning, organizing, and controlling. After the exercise, have them consider the following questions:

* What challenges did you face? How did you overcome them?

* What were some of the tradeoffs?

* What factors were critical in the amount of success you achieved?

* What distinguished the more profitable teams?

* What were the costs of profitability on the organization?

* What one thing would you have changed (i.e., less people, an additional resource)?

✓ ANSWERS TO CASE APPLICATION QUESTIONS

1. *If you were the mayor, what questions would you be asking?*

   I'd want a budget, broken down by department, that included budgeted expenses compared with actual expenses. I'd want to know what sort of systems are in place, and how much it would take to put new systems in place.

2. *Describe the type of feedforward, concurrent, and feedback controls you would install if you were the mayor.*

   A possible feedforward control would be an initial meeting with department managers when budgets are proposed to discuss their rationale. A possible concurrent control would include periodic follow-up meetings. A possible feedback control would include a written report or oral session revising the budgets or explaining what expenses budgeted or used were unreasonable and why.

✓ **SUGGESTIONS FOR USING VIDEO CASE**

"Health-Care Controls"

Running Time: 14:55

The whole issue of health care is one that is popular and current. This video case provides a frightening look at one aspect of health care—that of controlling for problem employees. The video looks at temporary nursing agencies and how they have filled a desperate need. However, in filling this need, these agencies often have to rely on questionable employees.

This video case could be used at any point in the chapter. In order for students to identify the types of controls that should be implemented in these agencies, you might want to wait until you have discussed the chapter information to use it. You could also have students do some additional research on the area of temporary nursing care to broaden their knowledge of the problems and challenges that are being faced.

ANSWERS TO QUESTIONS

1. *Should the government place regulations on temporary nursing agencies? If so, what types of controls should be implemented?*

   Students will have different feelings about whether or not the government should impose regulations on this industry. Those who feel that the government should get involved will probably cite personnel controls as being one important type of control to be implemented. Those who feel that the government should stay out of the industry will probably state that the marketplace will take care of any problem organizations by not purchasing their services.

2. *Assume you are a hospital administrator. Specifically describe the control system you would implement to protect your hospital against hiring people like Joe Akin.*

   The selection process would be an important part of a control system designed to prevent against hiring people like Joe Akin. Specifically, this selection process should have a system of reference checks and education/background checks to ensure that this type of person is not hired.

CHAPTER 16   CONTROL TOOLS AND TECHNIQUES

✓ LECTURE OUTLINE

✓ ANNOTATED OUTLINE

I. **INTRODUCTION** — p. 367

Understanding the operations side of an organization is important for comprehending how efficiency, productivity, and controls contribute to that organization's success.

Notes:

II. **INFORMATION CONTROL SYSTEMS** — p. 368

Management information systems are important tools in the manager's repertoire. The MIS is already affecting the manager's job and changing organizational communication.

A. A **management information system (MIS)** is a system that provides management with needed information on a regular basis.

Notes:

B. An **end-user** is the person who uses information and assumes responsibility for its control. When the manager becomes an end-user, he or she takes responsibility for information control. Managers are not becoming end-users because of the decentralization of information control.

Notes:

C. Managers are able to communicate through **networks**, the way of linking computers so the users can interact.

Notes:

_____

_____

_____

_____

D. **Planning.** Many companies have found that using a technologically-advanced information system can add to their competitive advantage. However, it is also important to sustain that information advantage.

Notes:

_____

_____

_____

_____

E. **Decision making.** An effective MIS will improve management's decision-making capability because it can provide both quality and quantity of information.

Notes:

_____

_____

_____

_____

F. **Organization structure.** Sophisticated information systems are reshaping the design of organizations. Managers can now handle more subordinates and organizations are becoming more organic without any loss in control for managers.

Notes:

_____

_____

_____

_____

III.   **OPERATIONS CONTROLS** — p. 374

Operations management is defined as the design, operation, and control of the transformation process that converts resources into finished goods and services.

A.   The **transformation process** is the process through which an organization produces goods or services.

Notes:

_____

_____

_____

_____

B.   **Cost control** is an important part of controlling operations. Many organizations have adopted a *cost-center* approach which is using units where managers are held responsible for all associated costs. Costs are made up of two types: *direct costs*, which are costs incurred in proportion to the output of a particular good or service; and *indirect costs*, which are costs that are largely unaffected by changes in output.

Notes:

_____

_____

_____

_____

C.   **Purchasing control** which involves monitoring the flow of inputs. Some aspects of this type of control are described next.

1.   *Building close links with suppliers* is an important step in developing effective purchasing controls.

2.   *Economic order quantity model* (EOQ) is a technique for balancing purchase, ordering, carrying, and stockout costs to derive the optimum quantity for a purchase order.

3.   *Inventory ordering systems* can either be a fixed-point or a fixed-interval type.

   a.   *Fixed-point reordering* is a system that "flags" the fact that inventory needs to be replenished when it reaches a certain level.

   b.   *Fixed-interval reordering* is a system that uses time as the determining factor for reviewing and reordering inventory items.

4. *Just-in-time* inventory is a system in which inventory items arrive when they are needed in the production process instead of being stored in stock.

Notes:

_____

_____

_____

_____

D. **Maintenance control** is involved with maintaining the equipment used in the transformation process. There are three approaches to maintenance control.

1. *Preventive maintenance* is maintenance performed before a breakdown occurs.

2. *Remedial maintenance* is maintenance that calls for the overhaul, replacement, or repair of equipment when it breaks down.

3. *Conditional maintenance* is maintenance that calls for an overhaul or repair in response to an inspection.

Notes:

_____

_____

_____

_____

E. **Quality control** is another area of operations control that is important to the manager. There are four factors that need to be considered in determining the amount and type of quality control.

1. *Acceptance sampling* is a quality control procedure in which a sample is taken and a decision to accept or reject a whole lot is based on a calculation of sample risk error.

2. *Process control* refers to sampling done during the transformation process to determine whether the process itself is under control.

3. *Attribute sampling* is a quality control technique that classifies items as acceptable or unacceptable on the basis of a comparison to a standard.

4. *Variable sampling* is a quality control technique in which a measurement is taken to determine how much an item varies from the standard.

_____

_____

_____

_____

V.   **FINANCIAL CONTROLS** — p. 381

Financial analyses serve as feedback controls.

A.   **Ratio analyses** enable managers to keep track of the organization's performance.

1.   Liquidity ratios

  a.   The *current ratio* is an organization's current assets divided by its current liabilities.

  b.   The *acid test ratio* is an organization's current assets, minus inventories, divided by its current liabilities.

2.   Leverage ratios

  a.   The *debt-to-assets ratio* is the total debt divided by total assets.

  b.   The *times-interest-earned ratio* is profits before taxes divided by total interest charges.

3.   Operating ratios

  a.   The *inventory turnover ratio* is revenue divided by total inventory.

  b.   The *total assets turnover ratio* is revenue divided by total assets.

4.   Profitability ratios

  a.   The *profit-margin-on-revenues ratio* is net profit after taxes divided by total revenues.

  b.   The *return-on-investment ratio* is (revenues divided by investments) times (profit divided by revenues).

Notes:

_____

_____

_____

_____

B. An **audit** is a formal verification of an organization's financial statements. It can be *external*, conducted by an independent source, or *internal*, conducted by an organization member.

Notes:

_____

_____

_____

_____

C. **Cost-benefit analysis** involves the evaluation of an activity where costs are known, but where the standard against which these costs must be compared is ambiguous or difficult to measure.

Notes:

_____

_____

_____

_____

D. **Activity-based accounting (ABC)** is an accounting procedure whereby costs are allocated based on activities performed and resources used.

Notes:

_____

_____

_____

_____

VI. **BEHAVIORAL CONTROLS** — p. 384

A. **Performance appraisal** is defined as the evaluation of an individual's work performance in order to arrive at objective personnel decisions. There are six major performance appraisal methods.

1. *Written essays method* is a performance appraisal technique in which an evaluator writes out a description of an employee's strengths, weaknesses, past performance, and potential, and then makes suggestions for improvement.

2. *Critical incidents method* is a performance appraisal technique in which an evaluator lists key behaviors that separate effective from ineffective job performance.

3. *Graphic rating scales method* is a performance appraisal technique in which an evaluator rates a set of performance factors on an incremental scale.

4. *Behaviorally anchored rating scales (BARS) method* is a performance appraisal technique in which an evaluator rates employees on specific job behaviors derived from performance dimensions.

5. *Multiperson comparison method* is a performance appraisal technique in which individuals are compared to one another.

   a. The *group order ranking* groups employees into ordered classifications.

   b. The *individual ranking* ranks employees in order from highest to lowest.

   c. *Paired comparisons* compare each employee to every other employee and rate him or her as superior or weaker of the pair.

6. Accomplishment of *objectives* can also be used, such as that done in an MBO program.

Notes:

_____

_____

_____

_____

B. **Discipline** refers to actions taken by a manager to enforce the organization's standards and regulations. The most common types of discipline problems involve attendance, on-the-job behaviors, dishonesty, and outside activities.

1. The *"hot-stove" rule* refers to the set of principles that can guide a manager in effectively disciplining an employee.

2. An effective selection process, acceptance of the organization's culture, a high degree of formalization, and employee training will reduce the likelihood that discipline will be necessary.

3. The selection process should screen out candidates who are likely to behave in ways contrary to the organizational values.

4. Employees who do not support the organizational culture are not likely to be employed long.

5. Formalization makes sure that employees are aware of what type of behavior is accepted and what type is not.

6. Through orientation and training, management lets employees know what the preferred work behaviors and attitudes are.

Notes:

_____

_____

_____

_____

✓ Answers to Review and Discussion Questions

1. *How can an MIS assist a manager in the control function?*

   MIS provides managers with more current information that can be more easily manipulated. It is changing the manager's job. MIS requires managers to have hands-on capability, will improve the manager's ability to make decisions, will expand the number of subordinates the manager can supervise, will lessen the power of middle managers, and will change the supervisor's job.

2. *In what ways is information a unique resource for organizations? Give examples.*

   Information is a unique resource in that it can be used for building power bases, is in abundant supply if used properly, and is relatively cost free. Some examples of information as a unique resource include the data bases that catalog firms utilize for direct marketing, Wal-Mart's use of an information system that gives them instantaneous information about company activities, and American Airlines' SABRE system of airline reservations that it also uses as a source of revenue.

3. *How can an MIS create a flatter organization while simultaneously giving managers more control over the organization's operations?*

   MIS gives managers more control by giving them more and better information. At the same time, however, it speeds up processes and can necessitate decentralization because more decision are being made at a faster speed. Flatter organizations can therefore become necessary to keep pace.

4. *Does the use of MIS empower all employees, all managers, or only a select few individuals in the organization? Discuss.*

   The use of MIS should empower all employees since information will be readily available to everyone within the organization.

5. *What is the transformation process?*

   The transformation process is the process through which an organization produces goods or services.

6. *Contrast acceptance sampling and process control.*

Acceptance sampling is a quality control procedure in which a sample is taken and a decision to accept or reject a whole lot is based on a calculation of sample risk error. It focuses on the product/service. Process control is a control procedure in which sampling is done during the transformation process to determine whether the process itself is under control. It focuses on the process.

7. *Which is more critical for success in organizations—total quality management or quality control? Support your position.*

Total quality management is important because it is all-encompassing. It is more of a general way of thinking than specific guidelines. In addition, it is about preventing errors in the first place, whereby quality control is about fixing errors and making sure that standards are met. Still, quality control is also important because it gives you a way to measure the results of quality endeavors.

8. *What are the more popular financial ratios and how are they calculated?*

The *current ratio* is an organization's current assets divided by its current liabilities.

The *acid test ratio* is an organization's current assets, minus inventories, divided by its current liabilities.

The *debt-to-assets ratio* is the total debt divided by total assets.

The *times-interest-earned ratio* is profits before taxes divided by total interest charges.

The *inventory turnover ratio* is revenue divided by total inventory.

The *total assets turnover ratio* is revenue divided by total assets.

The *profit-margin-on-revenues ratio* is net profit after taxes divided by total revenues.

The *return-on-investment ratio* is (revenues divided by investments) times (profit divided by revenues).

9. *"Cost-benefit analysis is better than no analysis at all. If the data are subjective and do lend themselves to objective analyses, cost-benefit provides at least a 'good enough' response." Do you agree or disagree with the statement? Explain.*

Cost-benefit analysis does not provide much in the way of concrete results. However, it is a measure. In addition, because standards are often vague, it adds a degree of flexibility. It doesn't offer a final answer, but it does provide insight into relatively how well an activity is doing from a particular perspective.

10. *What qualities would characterize an effective disciplinary program?*

An effective disciplinary program would follow the "hot stove" rule. Using this as a guideline, disciplinary action would be handled progressively, giving attention to mitigating circumstances.

✓ SUGGESTIONS FOR DISCUSSING BOXED MATERIAL

What's Wrong with Pirating Software?: The material is a good way to get into a discussion about the computer software industry. What is the law with regard to software (i.e., one legal copy for every computer the software is installed on)? Is this the same in the workplace? What if you want to take work home with you, but don't want to buy another copy of the software? Can you uninstall it every night, take it home with you, then reinstall it in the morning? Why is the law the way it is? How do software companies handle the situation (i.e., they build expected losses from piracy into the cost)? So, who's hurt?

Walter Forbes at Comp-U-Card: As a customer, how do you feel about companies gaining so much information about you? As a manager, how do you handle customer concerns about their eroding privacy?

Disciplining Employees: Is it necessary to have standard, organization-wide disciplinary procedures? As a manager, how do you maintain the appearance of fairness relative to other managers? How would you handle a disciplinary matter?

✓ SUGGESTIONS FOR THE SELF-ASSESSMENT EXERCISE

This self-assessment exercise focuses on discerning students' knowledge of Japanese manufacturing. The topic of Japanese management and manufacturing is usually of interest to students just because they heard so much about it from the news and business media. Have students complete the exercise and score it. Then have them answer the following questions as part of teams or individually:

* Were you surprised by your score? Why or why not?

* What does your score tell you about your knowledge of Japanese manufacturing techniques?

* If you are not pleased with your knowledge about Japanese manufacturing techniques, what could you do to improve it?

✓ COMMENTS ON CLASS EXERCISE

The purpose of this exercise is to give the students practice reading financial data. Here are the ratios:

current ratio:	1.16	2.07
acid test ratio:	.89	1.09
debt-to-assets ratio:	.46	.53
times-interest-earned ratio:	.92	3.62
inventory turnover ratio:	25.49	2.29
total assets turnover ratio:	1.59	.75
profit-margin-on-revenues ratio:	.02	.10
return-on-investment ratio:	.15	4.60

After the exercise, you may want to ask the following questions:

* What ratios did you find most useful in making your investment decision?

* Which ratios were the most difficult to interpret ?

* What other information would you like before deciding whether or not to invest?

✓ ANSWERS TO CASE APPLICATION QUESTIONS

1. *What TQM concepts did Harley-Davidson utilize as part of its turnaround?*

   In successfully implementing its turnaround strategy, Harley-Davidson utilized the following TQM concepts: just-in-time inventory, employee team empowerment, close relationship with suppliers, and quality control techniques.

2. *What specific types of controls did Harley-Davidson implement? How do you think each of these controls contributed to Harley-Davidson's turnaround?*

   Inventory controls are one type of controls that Harley-Davidson used. These controls eliminated the need for mountains of costly inventory. Quality controls were also used by employees and contributed to better products rolling off the production line. Undoubtedly, some types of cost controls also were utilized to help the organization keep its costs in line.

3. *What lessons can be drawn from Harley-Davidson that might help a company, like General Motors, that has seen its market share erode?*

   The lessons that Harley-Davidson can teach include the willingness to change and try something new. Harley-Davidson managers recognized that the old ways of doing things were not going to be successful any longer. They were not afraid to challenge the "status quo" and totally revamp the organization's operational and managerial systems. General Motors should take heed!

✓ SUGGESTIONS FOR USING VIDEO CASE

"Virtual Reality: Applications for Management?"

Running Time: 12:17

This video case illustrates an unusual development in the area of computer technology, that of virtual reality. The concept itself is hard to imagine and yet exactly what virtual reality does is imitate and stimulate the imagination. Most of your students will enjoy hearing about the potential benefits and challenges that virtual reality presents to organizations and managers.

The video case probably is best used at the end of the chapter material. At this point, students will have had an introduction to the area of computer technology, and hopefully, a stronger appreciation for the unique aspects of virtual reality.

ANSWERS TO QUESTIONS

1. *What specific management applications can you identify for virtual reality? Elaborate on each.*

    Student responses to this question will vary. Possible applications they might propose include: new product development and testing; physical space arrangements for offices; factory or office building layouts; advertising and other marketing tool development.

2. *What ethical dilemmas, if any, could you envision for managers who use this technology?*

    Like any type of technological advance, if virtual reality is used for illegal purposes, then questions of ethics also would arise. In fact, any use of virtual reality for questionable purposes would create ethical dilemmas for managers.

3. *How is virtual reality the ultimate MIS? Conversely, how could virtual reality completely isolate a manager from the important day-to-day realities of business?*

    Virtual reality could be the ultimate MIS because **any situation** could be manipulated and information acquired. However, these same qualities could completely isolate a manager because of his or her feelings. Why bother with the "real" facts when I can get information from a virtually-real situation?